# THE
# PORTABLE
# PUNDIT

# THE PORTABLE PUNDIT

## A Crash Course in
## Cocktail Party Conversation

### T. E. Krieger

**WARNER BOOKS**

A Time Warner Company

Copyright © 2000 by Todd Krieger
All rights reserved.

Warner Books, Inc.
1271 Avenue of the Americas, New York, NY 10020
Visit our Web site at www.twbookmark.com
Ⓦ A Time Warner Company

Printed in the United States of America
First Printing: October 2000
10 9 8 7 6 5 4 3 2

Library of Congress Cataloging-in-Publication Data
Krieger, T.E. (Todd E.)
    The portable pundit: a crash course in cocktail
    party conversation/by T.E. Krieger.
        p. cm.
    Includes bibliographical references.
    ISBN 0-446-67567-9
      1. Conversation. I. Title.

BJ2121 .K75 2000
302.3'46—dc21

                                            00-032493


*Cover design by Diane Luger*
*Cover illustration from CSA Archive*
*Book design and text composition by Fenix Design, Inc.*

For my Parents

# ACKNOWLEDGMENTS

*The Portable Pundit* was a highly collaborative project requiring the wisdom and knowledge of any number of specialists, all of whom I would like to give their due. Before doing that, I would like to thank my agent Laura Dail for thinking of me when this idea came her way, as well as for being an unflagging bastion of support. I also owe a debt of gratitude to my editor Caryn Karmatz Rudy, who showed me more patience than I deserved, and without whom this book would never have been initiated, let alone completed.

During the research phase of the book, I interviewed and corresponded with folks around the nation. All of them generously shared their time, insight, and best lines, so a collective thank you is therefore extended to: Dean Blackketter, Matthew Butterick, Russ Daw, Jonathan Grotenstein, Michael Kaplan, Murray Korngold, Tod Lippy, Erik Migdail, Ethan Nosowsky, Ben Prince, Jon Ritter, Ben Silverman, and Bob Stutch. I also wish to thank Benjamin Lipman. Without him I would have never found the voice, and Monique Stauder for being an excellent partner in crime and explaining the mysteries of a sideways 8.

I would also like to thank my Uncle Dennis for all the gold-toe socks that I have borrowed from him over the years and my good friend Ellen Levin for being exactly that. And oh yes, I'd like to thank the World Wide Web, without which this book would have taken at least a decade longer and been far less comprehensive.

# CONTENTS

# CONTENTS

# PREFACE

It happens to the best of us: to young and old, rich and not so rich, beautiful and not so beautiful. Breezing through an evening of small talk, bantering away about seismic changes in Soviet foreign policy or the crisis of faith in a small Latin American country—you run into a Total and Complete Conversational Dead End.

It might have been caused by a synaptic misfire, or maybe the conversation had simply run its course. Either way, a moment of silence gives way to a moment of tension, and you find yourself saying something as artless as, "Will you excuse me, I think I need to grab another drink," or its cousin, "Pardon me, I'm being flashed the 'come-over-here-right-now' sign." And depending on the situation, be it an office party, Christmas with the in-laws, or perhaps the après-golf cocktail hour, it is a moment that can have devastating consequences.

*The Portable Pundit* was conceived with an eye toward injecting levity into these moments. It has been filled with bits and pieces from classical and pop culture, all carefully placed in a context of conversational patter, to be served at gatherings of people from all classes and walks of life. While the bons mots you will find may not cause people to mistake you for Henry Kissinger—or even Ben Stein, for that matter—they may provide you with a baseline from which to navigate the sometimes choppy waters of the twenty-first-century cocktail party.

Originally this book took shape as *A Flip Man's Guide to Western Civilization*, but, following months of research into the history of thought, art, sports, sex, music, and the written word, it became clear that information, in and of itself, would be of little value. Rather, to be useful, the nugget or factoid had to serve a higher purpose to engage (or disengage) whomever you might be speaking.

For purposes of illustration, allow me to relate something my uncle once told me.

My uncle was at a Manhattan cocktail party, the kind where, over canapés and Campari, artists and lawyers mingle with bankers and models and discuss the fate of Western civilization while a Lou Reed song plays in the background. At this party my uncle met a woman who said she was from London. And to this woman from London my uncle said, "The people sleep, sleep in the daytime . . ." (a lyric from the Talking Heads album *Fear of Music*).

To which the woman replied, "If they want to, if they want to . . ." (which, as it happens, is the next line of the song). Of the three responses my uncle's lyrical missive could have engendered, this one—hip consent—was the most positive, with the other two being total confusion and mild disdain. And it is in this way that this anecdote speaks to the aspirations of this work: to provide the slightly deft, politely ironic, marginally self-deprecating comment that just might move forward whatever conversation you might be having.

For the right allusion, wielded with élan and grace, can be a cultural passkey to elevate (or denigrate) the conversation. It allows entrée into all manner of secret societies of which you might like to be a member. And, while this book cannot give you The Top 1000 Allusions and When and Where to Employ Them, it can—and does—seek to paint the world in comfortable hues of associative riffs, below-the-radar subtleties, and assorted marginalia.

Now, when I say allusion, it includes all manner of references: from congressional committees ("I am not a potted plant")[1] to *Saturday Night Live* catchphrases ("No Coke, Pepsi") to cult rockumentaries ("These ones go up to eleven"). Between twenty years of schooling and however many years of TV watching, music listening, moviegoing, and book and magazine reading, we have enough shared culture to make getting to know each other relatively painless and, hopefully, fun.

The book is organized in what can only be called quasi-chronological order, beginning with cave art and moving on up to technology and the financial markets. The tone is conversational: it's not supposed to teach you everything you never learned in college but give you enough to get by in most circumstances and to truly shine in a few.

## But, Above All, Beware the Gore Vidal Paradox

I wouldn't be doing my authorial duty were I not to warn that there are dangers in blindly quoting other people: dangers that must be paid attention to, and that can best be summarized by invoking the Gore Vidal Paradox,[2] so named after the very embodiment of erudition, one Gore Vidal. The Gore Vidal Paradox states: If

---

1. Oliver North's attorney Brendan Sullivan, seeking to be recognized in court, mouthed these now famous words.
2. An offshoot of the Gore Vidal Paradox is the Spalding Gray Corollary, which states that you should at no point in time ever quote Spalding Gray, for it is not what he is saying that is particularly funny but rather his delivery.

you are Gore Vidal, you are empowered to say whatever you like with impunity, whether that be about how Jack Kennedy handled the Cuban Missile Crisis or the finer subtleties of gay pornography.

If you're not Gore Vidal, it's wise to exercise caution as to how grandiose you choose to make your statements. For even among friends, credibility is a precious commodity that must be earned. For this reason it's worthwhile to stay in the conversational sandbox—lines from movies and TV shows—before moving into the high-rise hijinks of deconstructionist art and literary criticism.

But this book was not written for Gore Vidal, and most of the quotes, assorted miscellany, and anecdotal musings are to be borrowed by one and all. If something in here appeals—whether it's a riff on why Jackson Pollock was the last of his kind or how Madonna and David Bowie share certain DNA—by all means steal away. For a crash course is only as good as its graduates make it.

Enjoy. Drive safely. And remember to drink a glass of water before you go to bed. You'll feel a lot better in the morning.

T. E. Krieger

# Art: It's Not Just
## for Aesthetes Anymore

"That's not a solar system. It is a potato."

—Painter Joan Miró to surrealist poet Paul Éluard

*It's easy to overdo it when you start "talking art." This doesn't mean you can't have fun along the way, and Art, if it happens to be your bag, can be funnier than Bill Murray circa* Stripes/Caddyshack/Tootsie. *However, you need to be* in *on the joke, and if you're not it's best to bow politely, as if meeting a Japanese businessman when you've run out of business cards, and be on your way.*

If you are at an upper-crust cocktail party, there may or may not be certain kinds of pictures on the wall that you could point to as watershed moments in Modern Art. This is why you will find that there are no visual cues in this chapter, as it wouldn't really be fair to give you a visual aid and then take it away, now would it?

The chapter is also weighted toward twentieth-century art, much of which tends to be more conceptual and cerebral. As Modern Art is more about *Ideas*, it is that much easier to "talk" about in the absence of the *Art Object*. (Phrases in italics are called out to suggest their import and may be repurposed at will. Every effort has been made to use them in the appropriate fail-safe context.)

## Pre-History

I'll Take "What Is the Earliest Evidence of Painting?" for $1,500. . . .

The Cave Paintings at Lascaux, in the Dordogne[1] region in southwest France. They're from about 15,000 or 17,000 B.C., depending on how much faith you put in carbon dating. As for looking at the art, *Technique, Perspective,* and *Use of Color* aren't really the point here. Though it is neat that they managed to use red, black, and yellow. *Subject Matter* (and age) is what's important about *Les Caves*, and that subject matter is horses, lions, mammoths, and woolly rhinoceroses. (They weren't too good at drawing people either.)

---

1. The Dordogne region is where all your friends and their parents go for cycling and walking tours. You eat, you cycle, you sleep, you get up and do it again.

This particular development suggests that art can be about our lives, that its purpose is to document our existence.

"Hey, I'm as into video art as the next guy, but what does watching five hundred gallons of milk spill across a hard-wood floor really have to do with me? The cave paintings at Lascaux are more pertinent."

---

»Venus de Milo *is the one without the arms: 150* B.C.

»Nike of Samothrace *is the headless one with the wings: 190* B.C.

---

## Be Skeptical

Eschewing accepted thought is one way to demonstrate a studied level of analysis. Take the notion of the Renaissance, for example. Suggest, as scholars have for years, that "the-Renaissance-as-a-mass-cultural-explosion" is nothing more than a convenient generalization.

Argue that fourteenth-century Italy was in line with earlier developments in the twelfth and thirteenth centuries, and, while advancements did occur, it wasn't merely Dark Ages, Dark Ages, Dark Ages—oh-my-God—the Renaissance! But rather one long evolution from cave paintings to Masaccio.[2]

---

2. Born in 1401—he's the booby-prize winner time and again in the great "When Did the Renaissance Begin?" sweepstakes.

## Know a Fundamental Moment in Art History and the Size of Its Impact

Take *Perspective*. Express wonder and delight at the notion of perspective being introduced in the fifteenth century. In a landmark move, Filippo Brunelleschi,[3] his follower L. B. Alberti, and schoolyard favorite Piero della Francesca began workshopping the notion of perspective through manipulation of vanishing points. Along with other Renaissance advancements like individual consciousness and the notion of art having a secular life as opposed to simply a religious one, throw in the idea that now, for the first time, art could appear to be three-dimensional.[4]

» *Donatello's* David *is the cute little boy with long flowing curls wearing a hat and arm bent at his side: 1450.*

» *Botticelli's* Birth of Venus *is the woman standing on the shell: 1485.[5]*

» *Michelangelo's* Creation of Adam *is the one where God seems to be reaching out to fill Adam with divine light: 1510.*

3. Brunelleschi was behind the dome at Santa Maria del Fiore in Florence—you know the one—right next to the Duomo.
4. Compare this workshopping to the idea of being a transgender biracial performance artist in the East Village protesting a change in the government's methadone program and you can see things have changed in the past 500 years.
5. Uma Thurman played Venus in the interminable film *The Adventures of Baron Von Munchausen,* further cementing her role as fin de siècle muse.

# Riff on the Connection between High Culture and Low Whenever Possible

The Teenage Mutant Ninja Turtles did more to popularize Renaissance artists than anyone since the Medici.[6] For a brief, shining moment at the height of the Go-Go eighties, everyone aged five to twelve knew the names of the four masters of the High Renaissance: Michelangelo (Buonarroti), Leonardo (da Vinci), Raphael (Raffaello Sanzio), and Donatello (de Betto Bardi), and for that you can thank two guys named Eastman and Laird.[7]

> » *Random Factoid 2B:*
>
> *The* Codex *(fancy word for Leonardo's notebooks) were written in mirror text—right-to-left and backwards. Despite reports to the contrary, this says more about his uniqueness, his sui generis, than any kind of X-Files-level paranoia that he may have been experiencing.*

> »Liberty Leading the People *is the one where the left breast is hanging out; by Eugene Delacroix, 1830.*

> »Raft of the Medusa *is the one where everybody's on a raft on a stormy sea; by Theodore Gericault, 1818.*

---

6. Three generations of Medici served as patrons to artists of the Italian Renaissance: Lorenzo de (The Magnificent), son of Cosimo de and father to Giuliano de, was the most prominent.
7. (Kevin) Eastman and (Peter) Laird, the creators of the Turtles. Both are unimaginably wealthy, and Eastman is married to B-movie star Julie Strain.

|  | RENAISSANCE ARTIST | TEENAGE MUTANT NINJA TURTLE |
| --- | --- | --- |
| DONATELLO | REMEMBERED FOR: That cute little bronze David<br>CONSIDERED: Most influential of the Renaissance artists<br>LOG-LINE: Instilled *Emotion* into classical statues | FAVORITE COLOR: Purple<br>FAVORITE BOOK: *A Brief History of Time*, Stephen Hawking<br>WEAPON: Bo (Staff)<br>THINKS OF HIMSELF: As the Brains of the TMNT |
| LEONARDO | *Mona Lisa, Last Supper*[8]<br>Originates *sfumato* and presages Rembrandt's use of *chiaroscuro*[9]<br>LOG-LINE: The Ultimate Renaissance Man—scientist, inventor, painter, sculptor | GOES BY: Leo<br>FAVORITE COLOR: Blue<br>THINKS OF HIMSELF: As the Leader |
| MICHELANGELO | *David*<br>The Ceiling of the Sistine Chapel[10]<br>LOG-LINE: Goethe may have put it best: "Until you have seen the Sistine Chapel, you can have no adequate conception of what man is capable of accomplishing." | FAVORITE COLOR: Orange<br>LIKES: Surfing, rap music, video games<br>THINKS OF HIMSELF: As the Party Guy |

| | RENAISSANCE ARTIST | TEENAGE MUTANT NINJA TURTLE |
|---|---|---|
| RAPHAEL | *The School of Athens*<br>Log-Line: When the pope asks you to decorate his private apartments, you pull out your best stuff. | Favorite color: Red<br>Likes: Golf<br>Thinks of himself: As the Cynic |

8. Opportune moment to discuss the notion of permanence in art. The technique of oil painting used by da Vinci had caused this painting to deteriorate in his lifetime.

9. Chiaroscuro (kee-YAR-oh-SKYOR-oh) and sfumato (sfoo-MAT-oh) are generally reserved for discussing the paintings of the Old Masters, and as such tend not to have much of a life in casual conversation. However, as food presentation has become increasingly complex and dining itself an art, it is certainly within reason to utilize these terms in describing the minutiae of your dinner plate.

   Chiaroscuro—the balance of light and shadow in a picture and the skill shown by the painter in the management of shadows. Sfumato ("evaporated or cleared like mist")—transitions of color or tone from light to dark by stages so gradual as to appear imperceptible.

10. The restoration of the Sistine Chapel, executed over a ten-year period, a sure-fire hot-button topic. Not quite on the level of Ted Turner colorizing *Casablanca*, but long-standing questions remain about authenticity of restoration, primarily due to the new vibrant colors following restoration and whether or not those colors truly reflect Michelangelo's chosen palette.

# Have Something More to Say about Impressionism Than "Have You Been to the Musée d'Orsay?"[11]

## Modern Art Begins Here

Many people think of Modern Art as wacky stuff they can't understand and don't really like, and that their five-year-old nephew could create in an afternoon of free play. It ain't necessarily so. And you need look no farther than the visceral pleasures of Impressionism[12] to see where the above logic falls apart, for it is Impressionism that best serves as a starting point for all this "Modern Art" stuff. Five hundred years of literal representation begins to fall apart in the 1860s, as Impressionism gains steam.

> »Le Déjeuner sur l'Herbe *is the one with the nude chick on the grass and the two dudes beside her; by Édouard Manet, 1862–63.*

If you want to get into the semantics of it, you can talk about whether Impressionism was a *Style* (as is often suggested, perhaps wrongly) or a moment in time. The name

---

11. The Musée d'Orsay at 1, rue de Bellechasse in Paris, France, continues to top the list of Greatest Number of Visitors So Blindly Hungover They Couldn't See Straight, much as it has since opening in December 1986. While the Rijksmuseum in Amsterdam remains a tight second, the Frank Gehry–designed Guggenheim in Bilbao, open for business since 1998, has secured third and is moving up this cosmopolitan chart "with a bullet."
12. Actually takes its name from the Monet painting *Impression, Sunrise.*

stems from the idea that the artist wished to make "an impression" of what he or she saw, as opposed to an image.

The Impressionists (Claude Monet, Alfred Sisley, Pierre-Auguste Renoir, Mary Cassatt, and Gustave Caillebotte, to name but a few) were strongly influenced by photography, which arrived at about the same time, in two ways. The outdoor nature of photography enlightened the Impressionists as to the creative possibilities of working outdoors. So they up and moved to go paint in the great outdoors, or *en plein air* (a radical move at the time). Photography, with its focus on the image, also spurred the Impressionists to move beyond this concept of "image" and show how painting could be different and possibly even superior by dealing instead with the "impression" of the moment.

When you turn to Impressionism, talk about how you begin to see an acceptance of *Disorder* and *Discontinuity*, which eventually leads into Monet's *Water Lilies*.[13] Throw around the idea that this is a move away from *mimesis*— copying what you see—and more about painting how the subject seems or appears. And, of course, emphasis on the play of afternoon light in the great outdoors is always welcome. If you want to, talk about Impressionism as the moment when *Light* enters the picture.

## Impressionism as a Social Document

Impressionists are the first in a long line of artists' cooperatives to strike out on their own in opposition to the

---

13. Monet was respected more for his vision than his painting. As Paul Cézanne would say of him, "Only an eye, but my God what an eye."

mainstream.[14] While they didn't issue a manifesto per se (formalities of that kind came later), Impressionism is still the first movement to possess a group consciousness.

Of course, the Impressionists didn't entirely break with the bourgeois identity that defined art up to that time; Renoir continued to paint leisure-time activities like boating, which shows that they still believed in the luxuries of an upper class.

## Paul Gauguin (1848–1903) and the Importance of Chucking It All

The story of Paul Gauguin (Go-GAN) is a good one for cold winter nights when you're not sure just why you bother, for he is the patron saint for all those who wish they could just chuck it all and do something completely different. Following a meeting with Camille Pissarro in 1874, Gauguin took up painting and began exhibiting with the Impressionists. In 1883 he gave up his successful career as a Parisian stockbroker, forcing his wife to return to her family with their five children. He completed his journey from upstanding member of society to itinerant artist by heading out for the South Seas to live out his days painting in brilliant hues, blissed out among the natives of Tahiti.

---

14. Consider the possibility that Slamdance (the spin-off independent grass-roots film festival now held annually in Park City, Utah) is to Sundance (the official independent film festival held annually in Park City, Utah) what the Impressionists were to the Salon.

# Know That You've Got to Have the Code

Art can be enjoyed on a visceral level, but sometimes it's helpful to possess a little background information. Cubism is one movement that can make little or no sense without first having "the keys to the kingdom." In this case knowing that the *Theory* behind Cubism is the purposeful *distortion of perspective* in order to show all facets of an object is the difference between being informed and being clueless. Cubism is one of the first widespread instances of art that is not easily consumed by the average citizen.

## Collaboration in the Artistic Realm

Pablo Picasso's collaboration with Georges Braque as they mutually explored Cubism is considered one of the landmark partnerships in the History of Art. While there can be no doubting the magnitude of Picasso's influence on Art, it may well have been Braque who got the whole Cubist ball rolling, threw it over to Picasso, who messed around with it a bit and then threw it back. And so on. It was Picasso who said, "Bad artists copy. Good artists steal."

Refer to the relationship between Braque and Picasso—founders of Cubism—as a "marriage." Picasso certainly did.

## » What's It to You:

Consider the possibility of aspiring to be like Braque and Picasso rather than Butch and Sundance.

# Understand the Impish Nature of Marcel Duchamp

The wheels began to come off the proverbial cart in 1913 when Marcel Duchamp stuck a bicycle tire on a stool and pronounced it art. They came off for good in 1917, when he took a urinal, slapped the name R. Mutt on it, and presented it as art. Depending on where you sit along the Art Appreciation Continuum, you can choose either to revel in the irony that this urinal/sculpture is called *Fountain* or throw up your arms and say "Huh!?"

Duchamp also serves as a lightning rod for the whole "Is he serious?" discussion. In the latter half of the twentieth century, that is the usual tenor of the conversation surrounding the work of Jeff Koons.[15] (A Wall Street banker turned artist who may or may not be remembered for any number of ignominious art pieces—from a sculpture of Michael Jackson and his chimp Bubbles to a football-stadium-sized Chia Pet puppy).

Art that is conceptually playful may be referred to as *Duchampian.*

> *Duchamp called the bicycle wheel/stool and the urinal "ready-mades" because they were manufactured objects that he turned into art simply on his say-so, elevating them, as it were. And with this simple yet authoritative gesture he turned the entire Art world upside down.*

---

15. While much of Koons's work is open to the "Is he serious?" question, the high-quality large-format photographs of Mr. Koons having graphic sex with his then wife, Italian senator and pornstar La Cicciolina, may be considered the best example.

# Pablo Picasso Was Never Called an Asshole[16]

"When I was a child, my mother said to me, 'If you become a soldier you'll be a general. If you become a monk you'll end up as the pope.' Instead I became a painter and wound up as Picasso."—Pablo Picasso

Picasso was prolific, outspoken, celebrated, maligned, and by all accounts a misogynist.

Know too that he had a Blue Period, his creative periods mapped perfectly to his taking on of new mistresses, and more than anyone he lived la Grande Vie, was widely received throughout the world, splashed on magazine covers, and fabulously wealthy in his lifetime.

# Abstract Expressionism Was Willem de Kooning and Jackson Pollock

Willem de Kooning was driven by a burning desire to get the ineffable *It* across, a desire he shared with his comrade in *Action Painting* Jackson Pollock. And if you're ever in need of getting out of a conversation fast, tell a woman with whom you have been discussing art that there is something about her that reminds you about de Kooning's work, something that reminds you of *Women*. It's sure to free you up immediately. The violence of his canvasses is impossible to miss; he admitted they were "monsters" stemming not from an overt conscious act to defile but rather a yearning to express.

---

16. This is a line from a song by the Modern Lovers. It's a fine retort to nearly any comment relating, pertaining, addressing, or coming anywhere near Pablo Picasso.

» *Artists and the Female Form*

*The 1987 film* The Pick-Up Artist *was built around the following line: "Did anyone ever tell you that you have the face of a Botticelli and the body of a Degas?" Other possibilities include suggesting that a woman is long and lean as a Modigliani. But whatever you do, refrain from referring to someone as Rubenesque.*

## Three Things about Jackson Pollock You May Have Already Known

"The painting has a life of its own. I try to let it come through."                                        —Jackson Pollock

- He was a world-class drunk.[17]
- He pulled the canvas off the wall!
  And he put it on the floor![18]
- Contrary to popular notion, he wasn't gay.

Along with de Kooning, Pollock *was* Abstract Expressionism, which, if you're going to get into it, was the last time artists would take themselves so incredibly seriously. Wild with passion, seized by the desire to create, this movement was so dynamic as to be called *Action Painting.*[19] This was the last time someone would suggest that only through pure, feverish inspiration can

---

17. Pollock's alcoholism and the brilliance of his work are associated in much the same way that Charlie Parker's heroin habit and otherworldly saxophone playing are paired.
18. This move to the floor was as much of a milestone as when the Impressionists left their studios—and went . . . outside!
19. In Pollock's case this meant hurling paint forcefully from the brush with whipping motions—the brush never touched the canvas.

one create, that creativity is best defined as a frenzy you can't articulate.

This particular creative process was not in the least cerebral and can be summed up with a pithy French phrase, "Bête comme le peintre" ("Stupid like the painter"). This purist fiery notion of the painter has been crushed by every generation since.

---

## » *That Strange Relationship among Artist, Critic, and Buyer*

*"All profoundly original art looks ugly at first."*
—*Clement Greenberg*

*Art criticism came before Clement Greenberg, and it certainly came after, but few executed it with the style and conviction that Greenberg did. He not only supported Pollock wholeheartedly at a time when nobody else did, he also influenced Pollock's style directly—actually going by his studio while he was working and giving comments. Through his assertion that New York City was an international art center, Greenberg helped make the careers of Jasper Johns and Robert Rauschenberg as well.*

---

In his book on Modernism, *The Painted Word*, Tom Wolfe casts the art world as a triangle: the critic, the artist, and the unsuspecting public. As critic, Greenberg schooled the masses and in so doing paved the way for the artists he championed.

---

» *Jasper Johns is the one who did all those paintings of flags.*

» *Robert Rauschenberg pioneered Mixed Media.*

---

## Art Has Its Sexual Side

Little can suggest knowledge and familiarity with Art better than peppering psychoanalytic and sexual imagery into your Art Criticism. You can talk about Pollock as producing a kind of "hypermasculine art," a "jacking-off on a canvas," if you will, or equally, you can relate the story of the erased de Kooning.

As the story goes, a young Robert Rauschenberg went to see Willem de Kooning, who by this time was an established artist. Rauschenberg convinced de Kooning to give him a pencil drawing. Rauschenberg erased the piece (bold) and exhibited it as "Erased de Kooning" (bolder)—*by Robert Rauschenberg* (boldest). For full props, refer to this act as a desire to overcome the "anxiety of influence" and as being deeply Oedipal in nature, with Rauschenberg the son, and de Kooning the father.

It's a return to the fun and cerebral quality of Duchamp. It is the starting point for *Conceptualism*.

## Pop Art

*Andy Warhol:* Much in the way Louis Armstrong is remembered more for "Hello Dolly" than for his fundamentally changing the world of jazz, know that Andy Warhol really was an honest-to-goodness groundbreaking artist and you could do worse than spend time defending him.

If you were to choose to defend him, you might want to talk about how he understood the *aesthetic* of expendability. And about how he took the icons of American pop cultural life, Marilyn Monroe, Elvis

Presley, and Campbell's soup cans, to America and re-presented them to the public with a wry, "Hey, look again. It's art."

## Minimalism: It's Not What You're Making, It's What You're Using

When you talk about minimalism, understand that this term alludes to the absolute supremacy of *materials* over everything else, not necessarily a thin black line across a canvas. The *integrity* of the materials being used and the shapes that can be made supersede the importance of anything one may be trying to depict. So, rather than using art as a medium to evoke some kind of representation, you're interested just in the *properties* of the medium.

For example, take Richard Serra.[20] He's interested in iron: the weight of iron, the color of iron, the shapes you make with it. The weight, the very presence of a threatening, seven-ton sheet of iron, and the notion that it is perched precariously in the corner of a gallery translates into a mood. You can't help but consider the fact that this very heavy object is made of iron, that it's about iron, and iron is heavy. That it sits at an angle and it's a geometric form in the corner of a room, which is another geometric form.

---

20. Serra is one of the leading contemporary sculptors in the world.

# Conceptualism: Know How to Suggest That the Pencil Drawing on Your Napkin Is Worth Serious Money

Or at least if you were Sol Lewitt it might be. Sol Lewitt is known for presenting that the idea behind a work is more important than the work itself. The planning is more important than the construction, so he himself simply doesn't bother with painting. So when you buy a Sol Lewitt, what you get is a set of plans detailing specific geometric designs, and some assistants who will fulfill those plans. That's it.

## When You Talk of the Eighties . . .

. . . list the artists David Salle (SALL-ee), Robert Longo, and Julian Schnabel (SHNOBB-el) all in a row. When you talk of Schnabel, mention the heroic or romantic *content* of his work and how it was a *reaction* to the cool minimalism and conceptualism that preceded it. Be sure to mention that Schnabel's Neo-Expressionist style was easier to *consume* on a visceral level, making it the perfect art for the consumer-conscious eighties.

## And Though You May Want to, Don't Leave Out Christo

People may sometimes suggest that art should be dangerous, to which you could reply, "But not like Christo." Christo is that guy—you know the one—who wrapped bridges in plastic (Pont Neuf in Paris), buildings in fabric (the Reichstag in Germany), and surrounded tropical islands in collars of pink polypropylene (Biscayne Bay, near Miami, Florida). However, tragically, he once erected a series of immense umbrellas in the southern California foothills, one of which unfortunately blew over and killed a woman. Yes, art can be very dangerous.

## Women Can Play Too—Or Irony Isn't Just for Boys Anymore

Make sure to let it be known how impossible it is to talk about the eighties without talking about Cindy Sherman. And when you do, feel free to mention that you found her work difficult, possibly ugly, and certainly unpleasant, but remember that somehow it always sold.

---

### » Artists as Directors

*Whether it was coincidence or opportunity, celebrated eighties high-flyers David Salle, Julian Schnabel, Robert Longo, and Cindy Sherman[21] all went on to direct full-length feature films in the 1990s.*

*Scenario A: Call it the next level of bourgeoisie acquisitiveness, for what can a studio head buy after he buys a major piece of Art—but the Artist?*

*Scenario B: The New York art-world savants took their shows on the road to see if the same magic that worked wonders in the galleries of the eighties might work anew upon the silver screens of the nineties.*

---

21. David Salle directed *Search and Destroy*. Julian Schnabel directed *Basquiat*. Robert Longo directed *Johnny Mnemonic*, and Cindy Sherman directed *Office Killer*.

Using herself as a model, Sherman would pose for photographs in various wigs, taking on different roles from housewife to schoolgirl to vamp, all sharing the same enigmatic quality that left them open to interpretation. Looking for "multiple layers of complexity"? Look no farther and riff on her work and how it deals with psychoanalytic feminist theories, is art-history referential, and, for some, pornographic.

## Know on Which Side You Stand in the Culture Wars

In Literature you've seen it with James Joyce's *Ulysses* and Vladimir Nabokov's *Lolita*. In ballet you can always turn to Stravinsky's *Le Sacre du Printemps*[22] (*The Rite of Spring*), and there's never any shortage of outrage in Rock and Roll from Marilyn Manson to Ozzy Osbourne. But it takes a good Art Scandal to really stir the pot.

An overview of scandals of the recent past:

| ARTIST(S) | ORGANIZATION OPPOSED | ATTACKED WORK | OUTCOME |
|---|---|---|---|
| Damien Hirst | Society | Maggots swirling about a cow's head | Most fabulously popular of all his peers—the young |

---

22. Following the horrific reception of their masterwork, *Le Sacre du Printemps*, in Paris on May 29, 1913, Stravinsky and comrades in arts Diaghilev and Nijinsky adjourned to the Bois de Boulogne and wept.

| ARTIST(S) | ORGANIZATION OPPOSED | ATTACKED WORK | OUTCOME |
|---|---|---|---|
| | | | British Artists (YBAs). Hailed as the enfant terrible of the British, if not world, art scene. |
| Andres Serrano | Rev. Donald Wildmon | A photo of a crucifix submerged in urine Known as Piss-Christ | Serrano sent an image of Jesus dunked in milk—a white Christ—to Wildmon as a kind of appeasement. This didn't do the trick either. |
| NEA Four Tim Miller Karen Finley Holly Hughes John Fleck | Jesse Helms dubbed the "Ayatollah of North Carolina" by art critic Robert Hughes | Performance Artists: a woman smearing chocolate all over her body, a man urinating onstage, a lesbian satirist who writes things such as "the well of horniness," and, last but not least, the author of "My Queer Body" | After having their grants reissued (they were denied) the four found their lives unduly turned upside down, never to be the same again, and different not necessarily in a positive way. |

# The Most Expeditious Path to Getting Your First Drink

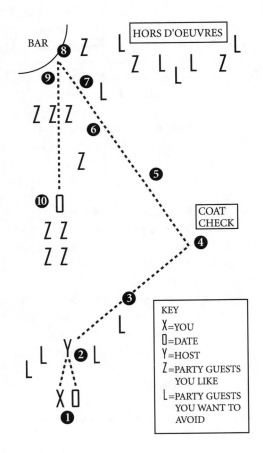

BAR

HORS D'OEUVRES

COAT CHECK

KEY
X = YOU
☐ = DATE
Y = HOST
Z = PARTY GUESTS YOU LIKE
L = PARTY GUESTS YOU WANT TO AVOID

# Timeline

1. **7:45 arrive.** Arriving earlier may force you to actually spend time talking with your host. Arriving later may force you to waste valuable time looking for your host before obtaining your first drink.

2. **7:48 greet host(ess) with date.** Introduce date to host(ess) **7:50** turn to date and say, "I think I'll go check our coats." Do not wait for reply.

3. **7:51 wave to "L" and smile.** Point to coats—show commitment to executing the task.

4. **7:53 coats checked.** Have singles always at the ready. This will facilitate your dropping off of coats and your exit.

5. **7:54 begin beeline** from coat check to bar.

6. **7:55 make eye contact** with good friend. Use sign language to indicate your quest for the bar.

7. **7:57 divert attention of "L"** by pointing to the hors d'oeuvre area and saying something like, "Look, fresh oysters. I hear they're an aphrodisiac" (repeat as necessary).

8. **7:58 smile at friends**—remain focused on obtaining drink (you can talk later).

9. **7:59 obtain drinks.**

10. **8:00 return to date** with drinks in hand.

# MYTHOLOGY FOR THE MAINSTREAM

*The oldest form of cultural referent
is the mythological story.
It's brief, colorful, and comes complete
with a simple moral lesson.*

## Cassandra

» The Drill:

The Greek god Apollo gave Cassandra a kiss. And with that kiss he gave her the power to see the future. With that same kiss he also took from her the ability to persuade, so nobody ever believed her.

» Why Cassandra:

Works for both sexes. When you know what's going to happen next, or have an inkling, but nobody will listen to you, referencing Cassandra might garner you a more attentive audience: "Look, I don't want to be a Cassandra, but Q4 does not look good."

## Icarus

Icarus—son of Daedalus—the inventor of the labyrinth.

» The Drill:

Icarus and Daedalus were imprisoned by King Minos for having given away the secrets of the labyrinth. In an escape attempt, they flew to freedom on wings made of wax, but Icarus—young, foolish, impetuous—flew too near the sun, his wings melted, and he plunged to his death in the sea below.

## » Why Icarus:

Icarus is not often mentioned by name, but the story, with its overtones of punishment for the overreaching zealousness of youth, has been a favorite for millennia. Whenever youth "goes for the gold," the story of young Icarus, the boy who flew too close to the sun, is invoked as a cautionary tale. "You know what happens when you fly too close to the sun. . . ."

# Morpheus

## » The Drill:

The original Mr. Sandman. Morpheus was the Greek god of dreams.

## » Why Morpheus:

Appropriate parting riposte: "See you in the land of Morpheus," or perhaps "Greet Morpheus for me."

# Narcissus

As in the root of "narcissistic."

## » The Drill:

As punishment for spurning the nymph Echo, Narcissus

was doomed by the gods to fall in love with his own image. Leaning over a pool of water, he saw his reflection, fell madly in love, and languished there until he died on the spot.

## » Why Narcissus:

Works mostly as an admonishment to vain (fe)male friends who insist on preening before the mirror. Think of it as a literate version of "Don't make funny faces or your face will stay like that."

# Sisyphus

## » The Drill:

Sisyphus was on the losing end of an argument with Zeus. His punishment was to roll a boulder up a steep incline for eternity, and to have it, at or very near the top of said incline, roll back down to the bottom, rolling over him or not, depending on how terrible a day he was having.

## » Why Sisyphus:

Because it's a good way to answer when somebody inquires into your employment, your life, or any really broad general inquisition: "Oh, you know, just pushing that rock up the hill." It implies a never-ending amount of effort with little or no gain. It puts your basic meaningless existence alongside the conflicts of the immortal.

# Architecture: More Songs about Buildings and Food

*Actually just more songs about buildings.*

*At the outer edges of conversational space—out by upcoming playwrights, beyond legendary jazz riffs, and just shy of contemporary philosophical discourse—is the "architectural conversation." It's not that architecture is not vital to our lives. It's simply that in the modern era, architectural speculation has become more refined and no crib guide, cocktail or otherwise, can arm you with the necessary historical, material, and philosophical underpinnings to defend yourself in a hostile forum.*

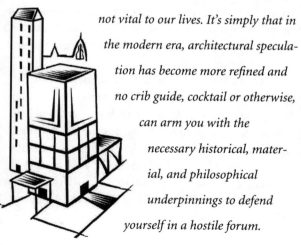

True understanding of architecture requires having handles on the concepts of personal *and* public space, geometry, and a pretty good feel for physics to comprehend the structural limitations of what you are looking at. While you're busy brushing up on that, think about these three things: how well (or not) the building fits into its environment, the materials it's made of, and what geometric forms—rectangle, triangle, circle, trapezoid—the building makes use of.

## From Pre-Historic to Present

Architecture has been with us since Day One. The moment the "lean" was put in a "lean-to," architecture was on the books. From there you can flash forward to the Greeks, who nailed the whole "two-posts-and-a-rock" thing, followed by the Romans, who invented the "arch" or "vault." And as far as columns go, if you don't remember your Doric, Ionic, and Corinthian, you've come to the wrong place.

Then man got obsessed with God and the Gothic style, and everybody was building "Houses of God" to honor the Almighty. All of which is very exciting in a junior-year-abroad kind of way, but for our purposes, much like we did with art, we're going to focus on the bonus round of Modern Architecture, beginning with Bauhaus and heading right up to the sparkling museum on the banks of the Bilbao River designed by the organically minded Frank Gehry.

# Nine Architects

Following are nine architects of the modern era, each chosen for a very specific conversational reason and presented in chronological order.

## Frank Lloyd Wright (1867–1959)

> "*Not only do I intend to be the greatest architect who has yet lived but fully intend to be the greatest architect of all time.*" —Frank Lloyd Wright, 1930

The variety of the work is impressive, from the sharp-edged corners of Fallingwater to the spirals of the Guggenheim in New York City. Frank Lloyd Wright may just be the closest thing to a rock star the field of architecture will ever see. He was a celebrity in his own right, appearing on TV with Mike Wallace and sharing his views on Nature and Organic forms. It is in that interview that he said of Marilyn Monroe, "I think Ms. Monroe is extremely good architecture."

As for his stylistic and philosophical views, Wright wanted to "destroy the box" and viewed the house not as a series of spaces but as one wide-open space flowing from room to room. He also believed that homes should blend into their environment and be made with local materials. If the backdrop was limestone, build with limestone. If red brick was what you would be sitting on, build with red brick. Nature (and he meant it with a capital "N") was his big baby.

## » The Take-Away:

Still the most important American architect of all time, and there's nobody sitting in the wings to claim that spot. His big thing? Cantilevers, it's all about cantilevers.[1]

Wow friends and neighbors by knowing that Wright designed the Marin County Civic Center, which served as the set for the film *Gattaca*. More important, know that if one must criticize Wright, it should be on the grounds that Fallingwater is falling apart. Yes, it was (and is) a phenomenal triumph of architecture, but a series of design decisions made by Wright himself have caused massive (and expensive) restoration plans to be undertaken.

And as a side note, should anyone be interested in building a mile-high tower in the city of Chicago, Frank Lloyd Wright has already drawn up the plans.

- *1909: The Robie House (the "Prairie Style"), Chicago*
- *1935: "Fallingwater," house for Edgar J. Kaufmann, Bear Run, Pennsylvania*
- *1937: Taliesin West, Home and School, Scottsdale, Arizona*
- *1956: Solomon R. Guggenheim Museum, final revised scheme, New York City*
- *1957: Marin County Civic Center, Marin, California*

---

1. **can-ti-le-ver** ('kan-tə-lē-vər) 1: a projecting structure, such as a beam, that is supported at only one end 2: a member, such as a beam, that projects beyond a fulcrum and is supported by a balancing member or a downward force behind the fulcrum

# Walter Gropius (1883–1969)

Gropius wasn't an architect of mind-boggling brilliance, but he was the mastermind behind the *Bauhaus* in Weimar, Germany. Literally translated as "house for building," the Bauhaus in post–World War I Germany served as a kind of epicenter for a specific manifesto-inspired architecture. Aspiring to be for the greater good (read: the worker), Gropius, and by extension the Bauhaus, sought to rid architecture of ornamentation and frills, which were considered bourgeois. The Bauhaus was keen on a revival of platonic ideas having to do with geometry and perfection, stripping away all ornamentation and extraneous decoration.

Gropius's big contribution? The relentless sameness of the International Style: white stucco, lots of glass, and some steel thrown in for good measure.

## » The Take-Away:

Along with Ludwig Mies van der Rohe (more on him in a minute) and Le Corbusier (him too), you can blame Gropius for all the glass boxes lining the streets of New York and Chicago. They so expertly conceived and presented their commitment to nonbourgeois ornamentation that the whole of America bought in.

On a personal note, Gropius was married to Gustav Mahler's widow, Alma, a fact that appears in any biography of him you may read. Alma has the distinction of being the first "art groupie" of the modern era.

- *1911: Fagus Works Shoe Factory, Alfeld, Germany*
- *1925: Bauhaus School and Faculty Housing,*
  *Dessau, Germany*

## Ludwig Mies van der Rohe (1886–1969)

Mies (it's a one-name thing) inherited the Bauhaus from Gropius and expanded upon it. Mies was all about the structural skeleton of a building; he didn't care much about the exterior. As far as materials go, he's the one who truly brought glass into vogue, pioneering internal structures that could support entirely glass buildings.

### » The Take-Away:

If you know one architect aside from Frank Lloyd Wright, it might as well be Mies. Throw around the idea that he created the modern vocabulary of architecture—the forms, their use, their interlocking meaning.

Mies also espoused a series of maxims that come in and out of vogue, but whether they are "in" or "out," it's good to know he's the one behind them.

*Less is more*[2]—An architectural pass at the KISS principle, "Keep It Simple, Stupid."

*God is in the details*—And you thought it was the devil? No, it's God, and Mies was committed to the details of his structures. His goal was to bring nature, man, and architecture together in a "higher unity."

*Form follows function*—It's all about bold, pure, simple forms that offer architectural integrity and structural honesty.

---

2. Robert Venturi, riffing on Mies's desire for simplicity, would suggest, "Less is a bore."

- *1929: The Barcelona Pavilion—It was subsequently destroyed but is considered a mecca for modern architecture.*
- *1959: The Seagram Building, Manhattan*

## Le Corbusier (1887–1965)

If Le Corbusier hadn't existed, somebody would have had to invent him. His real name was Charles-Édouard Jeanneret-Gris, but like all good artists he felt he needed his own pseudonym, hence Le Corbusier. (The in-the-know/pretentious of the world opt for calling him "Corb," "Le Corb," or "Corbu.") He was the archetype of the modern architect, down to his conservative dress and Coke-bottle-thick eyeglasses.

He thought a home was "a machine for living" and somehow managed to spend more time espousing his views at conferences and colloquia than building homes and office complexes. And as pointed out by Tom Wolfe in his acid-tongued *From Bauhaus to Our House,* the majority of his early commissions came from his family.

- *1929: Villa Savoie, Poissy—Le Corbu's highest achievement*
- *1958: L'Unité d'Habitation (Marseille, Nantes, and Berlin)*

## Philip Johnson (1906–?)

Originally schooled in philosophy, Philip Johnson's first major contribution to the field was as founder and director of the Department of Architecture and Design of the Museum of Modern Art—the first museum-affiliated program in the United States devoted to architecture as

Art. (And you thought *photography* had difficulty being recognized as legitimate.) In this capacity he and architectural historian Henry-Russell Hitchcock mounted a landmark exhibition, "The International Style."

Honoring Mies and Le Corbusier, the exhibition introduced a generation of American architects to their European counterparts and, as much as anything, can be held responsible for the shape of our nation's skylines.

## » The Take-Away:

The saying "Never trust an architect in a three-piece suit" may originally have referred to Philip Johnson. After getting behind the whole International Style thing (along with Mies he designed the Seagram Building), Johnson did an about-face late in his career (in 1984) with the AT&T building, which pretty much violated every tenet of all he had previously believed. Sporting an ornate top that has caused people to refer to it as "that giant Chippendale[3] in the sky," the AT&T building is a throwback to reviving historic styles, yet another no-no of the International Style.

And then there's Johnson's home, which you've probably seen a million times and never quite understood. It's a glass box in a field in New Canaan, Connecticut. A glass box, a brick floor, a steel frame—*c'est tout. C'est l'international!*

- *1949: Glass House, New Canaan, Connecticut*
- *1959: Seagram Building, Manhattan*
- *1984: AT&T Building, Manhattan*

---

3. Chippendale refers to Thomas Chippendale, who began the democratization of design with the publication in 1754 of *His Gentlemen and Cabinet Maker's Director.*

## » *The International Style*

*Spawned by Mies, Le Corbusier, and Walter Gropius, then championed and later practiced by Philip Johnson, the International Style is the dominant style of the mid-twentieth century. Earmarks of the International Style include the use of modern materials like glass and steel, a focus on structure combined with an emphasis on function, and furious opposition to decorative stylings. (International Style advocates for example are extremely put off by the Chrysler Building in Manhattan, with its art-deco accoutrements.)*

# I. M. Pei (1917–?)

Pei splits it down the middle, favoring the materials of the Gropius crowd—steel, glass, stone, and concrete—but getting funky with his shapes, and he has no concerns about commercialism. A free agent, Pei belongs to no specific camp and his designs always strongly showcase *Light* and *View*. He also champions the public space, as is evidenced in his design for Creative Artists Agency (CAA), with its giant atrium. (Oh come on, you've seen it before—every time they show CAA they show all those nice little agents in a gigantic, wide-open space.)

## » The Take-Away:

Call him the fun one. Pei has steered away from pronouncements of both academic and philosophical nature, preferring to let his work speak for him. He's something of a pop artist working in architecture, and you either love what he does or hate it. Just remember the Pyramids at the Louvre and you're set.

- *1968: National Gallery of Art, Washington, D.C.*
- *1983: Grand Louvre Pyramids, Paris*
- *1996: Rock and Roll Hall of Fame, Cleveland*

## Robert Venturi (1925–?)

The academic of the bunch. Venturi will inevitably be remembered more for his theories than his work. As the author of *Learning from Las Vegas*, Venturi claimed that architects could learn a lot from "the kitsch of high capitalism." Bringing a postmodern approach to everyday structures like an A&P parking lot, Venturi argued for "complexity and contradiction."

### » The Take-Away:

Just know that he wrote *Learning from Las Vegas*, the academic storming-out of the Ivory Tower, to declare "Architecture is dead; Long live Architecture."

## Frank Gehry (1929–?)

He's Canadian—that might explain some of it. With his seminal work on the Guggenheim Museum in Bilbao, Gehry has vaulted to the top of every list relating to architecture at the turn of the century. *New York Times* critic Herbert Muschamp referred to the Guggenheim as a "miracle" and said it had launched the clarion cry throughout the land, "Have you been to Bilbao?" He even went to so far as to suggest that it begged the question, "Has it become possible to talk about beauty as a form of truth?"

The Bilbao Guggenheim is *the* architectural creation of the nineties, if not of the past twenty-five years, and it is wildly heralded as such. If you talk of Bilbao—and you will—talk of the play of light on the titanium structure, how the building looks different from every angle from which you look upon it, and how much it makes the city, bringing the docks to life as opposed to making them look shabby.

To call Gehry an iconoclast would be putting it mildly. Liking to use unconventional materials, he is often considered more a sculptor than an architect.

## » The Take-Away:

Gehry is the go-to guy right now. Bilbao, built around the same time as the billion-dollar Getty Center in Los Angeles and San Francisco's Museum of Modern Art, has remained on the top of everybody's travel and architectural wish list. Understand Gehry to be idiosyncratic, very much a man of the people, and realize that he has a weird obsession with fish.

He also has worked in a nearly symbiotic relationship with Richard Serra, something that may have reached its apex with their work in Bilbao, wherein Serra has a permanent exhibition.

- *1978: Gehry House, Santa Monica, California*
- *1989: Disney Concert Hall, Los Angeles, California*
- *1997: Guggenheim Museum, Bilbao, Spain*

## Robert A. M. Stern (1939–?)

The second coming of the Academic. He's on this list for one reason and one reason only: the town of Celebration in Florida. He was the co-planner of this town created by the Walt Disney company.

### » The Take-Away:

Celebration is the real-life version of *The Truman Show*, the very picture of planned tranquillity and a return to Main Street America. Any conversations pertaining to "the gated community" may eventually turn to Celebration. Was it a success? Was it a failure? Know that Stern, currently the dean of the School of Architecture at Yale University, was the man with the plan and that Celebration is an ongoing experiment in planned living on a town-wide scale.

# Linguistic Interlude I: Latin

*It all starts and ends with Latin. So here's some to toss around freely.*

» *Flagrante delicto*
Getting caught with your hand in the cookie jar in legal terms.
More commonly, Latin for a more public form of intercourse:
"They were caught in flagrante delicto."

» *Persona non grata*
Having the status of no longer being welcome where you may
formerly have been welcome.

» *Quid pro quo*
Memorably invoked by Hannibal Lecter to Clarice Starling in
the film version of *The Silence of the Lambs*. "Quid pro quo,
Clarice, quid pro quo." Latin for "tit for tat." Might be used in
extensive drinking contests such as Thumper or Quarters,
wherein you force somebody to drink who has just made you
drink moments earlier: "Quid pro quo, Biff, quid pro quo."

» *Sui generis* (SOO-ee-JEN-er-is)
That of which there is only one. Michael Jordan.

# Philosophy for Philistines

"The only thing I know is
that I know nothing."

—Socrates

"The unexamined life is
not worth living."

—Socrates

*An overlooked feature of
Philosophy, at least as far as
the discipline relates to
appearing erudite, is that a
little goes a long way.*

# The Paradox of Philosophical Inquiry

Philosophy with a capital "P" can seem imposing: Those who casually let slip, "Oh yeah, I studied Philosophy,"[1] are often met with "oohs" and "aahs." But the beauty of attempting to appear knowledgeable in Philosophy is that once you get the basics under your belt, have a few of the key names to drop, and spend a moment thinking about what *they* thought about, you'll see that the only difference between you and the bigger minds out there is how *rigorous* they are in their thinking.

The history of Philosophy can be seen as a drawn-out intellectual skirmish with a seemingly interchangeable list of combatants—no clear winners, a few well-documented losers, and an incomprehensible amount of brainpower expended.

For even if your ass is hanging so far off a conversational cliff that you're thinking Wile E. Coyote had it *good*, a Socratic lift here and a Nietzschean reference there may just buy you enough time to scramble back onto terra firma. But before you bust out your copy of Aristotle's *Ethics* or go running for that dog-eared copy of Sartre's *La Nausée*, let's tackle the major branches of philosophical inquiry and their relevance (or lack thereof) to our lives today.

---

1. Actually a real live Philosopher consulted on this chapter said the following: "The typical reaction (particularly at parties) is along the lines of 'Oh, you studied philosophy? I'll bet you talk more shit than anyone!'"

# Five, Did I Hear Five?

Philosophy boils down to five essential branches of inquiry. And while some might suggest that advances in Physics, Biology, Chemistry, and Higher Math have made Philosophy irrelevant, your inner Philosopher should respond, "Discovering more about the mechanics of the brain hasn't really shed light on the tough philosophical questions regarding consciousness, now has it?"

## Inquiry Branch #1: Logic

Logic is Aristotle's bag, if you want to name names. He's the guy who gave us "the syllogism."

E.g.,

All men are mortal.

Socrates is a man.

Ergo Socrates is mortal.

Logic is something of a lost art, and though widely practiced in most centuries prior to ours, it has faded from the daily discourse, save for references to the Vulcan hero of *Star Trek*, Mr. Spock.

The very least you can do is to seek to define the term.

Try the following:

"Didn't I. M. Copi[2] say 'Logic is the study of the methods and principles used to distinguish good reasoning from bad'? Or something like that. That's what Logic is, right?"

---

2. I. M. Copi—One of the few modern-day logicians.

> ## » *Ergo*
>
> Ergo *is Latin for "therefore." Great when trying to point out somebody's shortcomings. Jack is late. Putzes are late. Ergo Jack is a putz. Ergo* sounds *less offensive than "therefore."*

> ## » *Logic vs. Rhetoric*
>
> *There is, of course, Rhetoric, which is any attempt at linguistic persuasion—short of explicit threats. Logic is the study of good reasoning; rhetoric is the study of all techniques that will persuade an audience.*[3]

## Inquiry Branch #2: Ethics

Ethics. Although they can be hard to find (Damn, where did I stow my ethics?), tricky to monitor, and slippery even when unearthed, ethics are (hopefully) an integral part of our lives. Were you to raise any of the following questions at an inopportune time—say, after the first bottle but before the third—you might be in for a very long night.

### Ethics' Place in the World

» Extremely Broad Ethical Questions:

Are there any such properties as right and wrong, good and bad? Is ethics just a matter of opinion?

---

3. For another "technique that will persuade an audience" refer to the "reality distortion field" belonging to one Mr. Steve Jobs, founder of Apple Computers.

I.e., Is killing an evil man ethically wrong?[4]

## » Somewhat More Narrow Ethical Questions:

How do we know what's right and wrong? Through intuition? By direct observation?

I.e., Can we *see* right and wrong, the way we see the color of a car?

## » And Somewhat Narrower Still:

Am I doing the right thing? Is this end good? And if the end is good, does it justify the actions?

I.e., Is working for a software company bent on world domination okay if your role at the company is to help inner-city children get on-line?

# Inquiry Branch #3: Aesthetics

Essentially, as many things do, this boils down to Pamela Anderson (Lee). Is she considered attractive because she represents some higher ideal of womanhood? Or rather because *Entertainment Tonight, Playboy* magazine, and twenty-five years of received culture have made it so? As the media society warps the notion of "taste" vis-à-vis "aesthetics," is it possible to believe that we, as individuals, can appreciate the aesthetic qualities of non-commoditized objects, or is "taste" merely a manufactured affinity?

If the Pamela Anderson Lee example doesn't resonate, think about the Top 40 song that "grew on you." On

---

4. In literature, this is the domain of Fyodor Dostoyevsky—to be specific his magnum opus *Crime and Punishment.*

some rainy day you find yourself enjoying a Mariah Carey song that you swore you hated. Was it because you began to understand the subtler meanings of the lyrics and the interplay between the hip-hop backbeats and diva song stylings? Or did you just get so beat up by MTV, *Entertainment Weekly*, and *SPIN* that you simply gave in to the court of popular opinion?

## Aesthetics' Place in the World

Aesthetics is the branch of inquiry to play around with in crowds of opinionated folk, and can be a fine way to comment on a friend's taste in music, clothing, and/or companionship. "Darling, all I can say is that his appreciation for those things that might be termed aesthetically appealing is questionable."

# Inquiry Branch #4: Epistemology

What is knowledge? How is knowledge different from mere opinion? What, if anything, can we know for certain?

# Inquiry Branch #5: Metaphysics

What exists? What is the relation between the mind and the brain? What is time? What is space?

## Metaphysics' Place in the World

Some say that Metaphysics has lost its place in the world, having been supplanted by more "concrete" sciences, but as a person concerned with philosophical inquiry, you might beg to differ, as evidenced in the following scenario:

PERSON A: Metaphysics, that's so nineteenth-century. We're discovering new galaxies, looking into the nature of time—black holes are being confirmed and we've got hard data on the galaxy expanding. And you talk of Metaphysics?

PERSON B: I wouldn't dismiss it so fast. Ask a physicist what causation is and she'll either have a poor answer and start looking for a philosopher ASAP or she'll have a rocking answer because she's done the requisite philosophical work (i.e., Science does *not* answer the bigger questions).

---

## » *Objective Truth*

*Over time the exploration of an "objective truth" has become the path least followed.*

*Dismissing "objective truth" came into vogue with pessimistic cigarette-smoking philosophers[5] in France who simply said, "Bah, I haff no need for the truth." (A statement that was usually accompanied by a dismissive sweep of the hand away from the body.)*

*But others have said that's too facile, rather, "Truth may be whatever we all agree on." Or at least that's what the very bright and talented modern-day philosopher-cum-literary-theoretician Richard Rorty said. And if you can't find "objective truth" or Truth with a capital "T," perhaps you might consider Rorty's definition as—well, true.*

---

5. To introduce moments of extreme levity into any heavy-duty philosophical discussion, one could posit the following: "Do you know what brand of cigarette Roland Barthes smoked— Gitanes or Gauloises?" It suggests a playful familiarity with the big-time structuralist and a willingness to be irreverent in the most serious of times.

## Of Philosophers and Concepts

The big philosophical questions tend to run along
similar lines; and philosophical name-dropping boils
down to knowing the contributions of various philosophers and how they do or don't play in Modern Times.

### The Virtue of Knowing Nothing
### Socrates (470–399 B.C.)

» His Bag #1:

The Socratic method:[6] Socrates' style of Q and A was
also known as the dialectic, and it was his way of getting
to the bottom of things. Infused with the humility that
he knew nothing, Socrates would, through diligent
questioning of all with whom he came into contact,
seek to understand the world.

» What's It to You:

Socratic humility—notion that it's okay that I know nothing can serve as a powerful antidote to fear and trembling
in large crowds. Use it as pep-talk material for friends ter-
rified to go into bars, nightclubs, and uptight parties.

"Pretend you're Socrates and you're on a quest for
truth."

---

6. The Socratic method bears a striking resemblance to Peter
Falk's turn as the trenchcoat-wearing, cigar-smoking Detective
Columbo, who returns time and again to the same question
with his annoying catchphrase, "Oh, and one more thing . . ."
Not to mention the Socrates-esque nature of Columbo's false
humility.

» His Bag #2:

Messy Public Death: Forced to drink a hemlock cocktail for the practice of spreading dangerous ideas.

» What's It to You:

Gallows humor. Having had a terrible day and not looking forward to the next, inquire of your host-/hostess-bartender if he or she could add a little hemlock to your beverage. "Ketel One Martini, straight up, three olives and a splash of hemlock."

# The Forms
## Plato (428–354 B.C.)

» His Bag #1:

Forms: Where Socrates was interested in human morality, Plato was concerned with understanding the Nature of the World. To Plato, all we experience are pale copies of pure ideas aka Divine Forms. These Divine Forms can't be seen, they can't be experienced, and they can be understood only through the power of the mind.

» What's It to You:

A true understanding of the concept of Divine Forms can serve as a great way to rationalize material desires. For example:

"A Range Rover and a Yugo may be two different reflections of the Form that is the Great Car, but the Range Rover most certainly is closer to the Divine Form—the Great Car. So really, baby, in buying the

Rover I'm working at living up to the Platonic ideal, and what could be more noble than that?"

## » His Bag #2:

*The Allegory of the Cave:* A group of people are in a cave. A fire burning behind them throws their shadows up on the wall. They see the shadows, and, having known only the cave and these shadows for their entire lives, mistake these shadows for "reality" just as people mistake what they see all around them for "reality" when in actuality there is sunlight and a whole different world to be experienced.

## » What's It to You:

Scenario A: Useful in attacking the rat race, living in Manhattan, the (perceived) necessity of accumulating great wealth, etc.

"Come on, you're like those people in Plato's Cave. You need to crawl out into the sunlight to see the bigger picture."

Scenario B: Score philosophy geek points for tying Platonic thought into mainstream pop culture.

"Yeah, *The Matrix* was visually stunning and those scenes with the bullets were mind-blowing, but it wasn't necessarily saying anything that original. The whole we're-trapped-and-there's-a-better-world-but-we-can't-conceive-of-it thing has been a live issue since Plato was talking about shadows flickering by firelight."

# Aristotle (384–322 B.C.)

» His Bag:

*Western Civilization*: He categorized everything that was then known, creating the divisions between areas of knowledge that have come to be known as Physics, Biology, Botany, Political Science, Anatomy, and in so doing laid the groundwork for what would eventually become Higher Education.

» How to Use It:

Posit whether Aristotle would agree with YAHOO!'s hierarchical trope.

» His Bag #2:

His pupil was Alexander the Great.[7]

» What's It to You:

Pondering the exchange between one of the world's great military minds and one of its leading philosophers has great comedic potential. What on earth could they have talked about? For example:

ALEXANDER: Ari, I'm off to invade Asia.

---

7. Ruling figures and their personal attendants remains a fertile area to explore. For example, consider the relationship between William Close (Glenn Close's father) and the African dictator Mobutu Sese Seko of Zaire. Close was Mobutu's personal physician. "Mobutu, you must really rest today," says Close. Mobutu's reply: "But Will, I must pillage and raze several villages. I cannot rest."

ARISTOTLE: But Master Alexander, you promised we would review the Pythagorean theorem and you've fallen far behind in your physics. I'm sure Mesopotamia can wait.

## To Be a Saint You Sometimes Need to Be a Sinner St. Augustine (354–430)

» His Bag:

*God, God, God, God, God, God, God*: Augustine is the first of the big-league philosophers to be a card-carrying member of the Modern-Day God Squad. Major accomplishments include writing the first modern autobiography, *The Confessions of St. Augustine*. To get a feel for the depth of Augustine's devotion, here's a snippet from the *Confessions*:

1.4.4

> What art Thou then, my God? what, but the Lord God? For who is Lord but the Lord? or who is God save our God? Most highest, most good, most potent, most omnipotent; most merciful, yet most just; most hidden, yet most present; most beautiful, yet most strong, stable, yet incomprehensible; unchangeable, yet all-changing; never new, never old; all-renewing, and bringing age upon the proud, and they know it not; ever working, ever at rest; still gathering, yet nothing lacking; supporting, filling, and overspreading; creating, nourishing, and maturing; seeking, yet having all things.

## » What's It to You:

He arrived at his sainthood via a wayward path that began with pear-stealing, wandered into brothel-attending, and stopped over in mistress-keeping and Manichaeism[8] before arriving at his "conversion" at age thirty-two. A useful role model for the sinner in all of us, as his one-eighty from sinner to saint can be pointed to as an example that there is hope for us all.
I.e., "Look at Augustine. Give me time."

## » Conversation Stopper:

Augustine believed that God created the world, but that posed a problem. IF God created the world, what on earth was the Almighty doing before? Augustine's answer: God is outside of TIME. He started time, or, if you prefer, he was around before time began. Throw this one out there when conversation about religion (which should be avoided at all costs) seems to be bubbling up to the foreground.

---

8. Manichaeism: The religion of Mani—and not as in Mani's Deli. Basically very into Good and Evil, not very into the mysteries of the Christian faith, much more involved with explaining *all*.

# I Think, Therefore . . .
# René Descartes (1596–1650)

» His Bag:

Descartes suffered from no lack of self-esteem. To arrive at *Cogito ergo sum*—"I think therefore I am"—he tossed everything that came before—God, Church, Aristotle—and started anew. He did so to reclaim certainty vis-à-vis all the things he thought he knew about the external world and restore confidence in our general scientific methods. He was seeking to prove that he had a right to claim that he knew anything.

In many ways he is comparable to the much-loved and self-absorbed comedian Jerry Seinfeld.

|  | DESCARTES | SEINFELD |
|---|---|---|
| Claim to Fame | Father of Modern Philosophy | Father of Post-Modern Sitcom |
| Catchphrase | *Cogito ergo sum.* | Not that there's anything wrong with that . . . |
| Approach to His Field | Do away with everything that came before and begin with Nothing. | Do away with everything that came before and make a program about nothing. |

|                      | DESCARTES                                                      | SEINFELD                                                          |
| -------------------- | -------------------------------------------------------------- | ---------------------------------------------------------------- |
| Intellectual Premise | All knowledge of external things is in the mind.               | All knowledge of external things is in Jerry's mind.             |
| Lasting Impact       | All scientific inquiry has followed in the steps of Cartesian doubt. | All television shows have followed in the vagaries of Seinfeldian nothing. |

## The Plight of the Modern Man
## J.-J. Rousseau (1712–1778)

*"Man is born free; and everywhere he is in chains."*
—Jean-Jacques Rousseau

» His Bag:

Rousseau said that primitive man—the Noble Savage— existed in a state of harmony, while modern man is cut off from himself. By the eighteenth century, existing as primitive man was not a viable option so Rousseau came up with an alternative notion suggesting that individuals, in order to achieve a more balanced and efficient state, enter into a Social Contract. In essence it is necessary to "buy in" in order to reap the rewards of Society.

## » What's It to You:

The Social Contract is a useful means of addressing participation in Modern Society. A tale of two lifestyles: the Luddite and the Corporate Warrior.

|  | THE LUDDITE | THE CORPORATE WARRIOR |
|---|---|---|
| Profile | He or she without computer, e-mail, cell phone and wireless devices—kin to the Noble Savage. In a "primitive state" and, theoretically, in harmony. | Cell-phone-clutching, stock-portfolio-watching, 97-e-mails-a-day-writing, plugged-in cybernaut. |
| Quote | "I don't care if I'm not living up to my end of the Social Contract; personal technology freaks me out and I think my life is just fine without it. . . . Better even." | "Look, it's my Job* to be this plugged in." *Job defined as a person in Society—not job as defined by fiduciary responsibility. |
| Extreme | IF TAKEN TO EXTREMES The Unabomber | IF TAKEN TO EXTREMES That guy on the plane seat next to you talking to the central office, running spread sheets, and evaluating his options package. |

## The Pleasant Skeptic Is Your Friend
## David Hume (1711–1776)

> "*What a peculiar privilege has this little agitation of the brain which we call 'thought.'*"     —David Hume

» His Bag:

Hume said that just because the sun rises every day doesn't guarantee that it will rise tomorrow.

» What's It to You:

A reason to get out of bed in the morning, as the possibilities, indeed, are endless.

A few modern-day examples as proof:

- Just because every time the Boston Red Sox go to the World Series they lose does not mean the next time they go to the World Series they will lose.
- Just because every time Charlie Brown flies a kite it gets eaten by the kite-eating tree does not mean that the next time he flies the kite it will get eaten by the kite-eating tree.
- Just because you have been stuck in a dead-end job since you graduated from college does not mean you will necessarily remain stuck in a dead-end job.

# The Categorical Imperative
# Immanuel Kant (1724–1804)

> "*Two things fill the mind with ever new and increasing admiration and awe, the oftener and the more steadily we reflect on them: the starry heaven above and the moral law within.*"
>
> —Immanuel Kant

## » His Bag:

Kant is often considered the greatest of modern philosophers. After having published regularly for much of his life, he took a decade off, 1770–1781, to write his masterwork, *A Critique of Pure Reason*. Kant is remembered for the Categorical Imperative.

It posited: A person should behave in such a way that if all people behaved in the same way the system would still hold.

I.e., You shouldn't commit adultery, not because it's against the Sixth Commandment, but because if everyone committed adultery, then there would no longer exist the institution of marriage and such a thing as "adultery" wouldn't exist. (The point here is trying to establish an ethical code on the basis of pure reason.)

## » What's It to You:

Kant's most famous example of the above is: You shouldn't break a promise when it is to your advantage or *the very institution of promise-making* would collapse.

» His Bag #2:

*On "What Is Stuff?":* Kant posited that we don't see things as they really are; they are "unknowable," and all our observations are mediated through what he called our "sensory manifold." As much as there is a substance within things, such as, say, a rock, it is mysterious.

» What's It to You:

Useful in setting limits on human comprehension. The idea that we can know only certain aspects of the physical world, that certain things just *are*, and that somebody as intellectually rigorous as Kant said so is just the right prescription to help anxious friends pondering the fate of the universe.

## Georg Wilhelm Friedrich Hegel (1770–1831)

> *"What experience and history teach is this—that people and governments never have learned anything from history, or acted on principles deduced from it."*

> —G. W. F. Hegel

» His Bag:

Hegel took himself *extremely* seriously. He created a total framework for understanding the Whole of Human History—past, present, and future. He took that bundle, intertwined it with the History of Thought, *and* argued that Thought and History have forever been inextricably linked throughout Time and will continue to be so until they reach the state of supreme self-consciousness—

the Absolute Spirit. All of this somehow added up to Hegel's proclaiming himself to be in touch with said Absolute Spirit, and, not lacking for subtlety, he claimed that the Prussian state in which he was currently living was, in fact, the end result of several thousand years of political development.

» What's It to You:

A facile way to show intellectual prowess is to be dismissive of earlier generations' Great Works. To this end, you might refer to the totality of Hegel's system—Thought and History all rolled up into one great big intellectual construct—as being "quaint."

» His Bag #2:

*Zeitgeist Has a Home*: More simply, Hegel gave us the term *Zeitgeist*,[9] literally translated to mean "time-spirit," pointing to the interconnectivity of individuals and art, society, and religion in a certain age. A twentieth-century figure most often fingered for best capturing the Zeitgeist is one Bob Dylan.

## Søren Kierkegaard (1813–1855)

> *"Life can only be understood backwards, but it must be lived forwards."* —Søren Kierkegaard

---

9. Many of the best examples of "What is Zeitgeist?" seem to come from the modern American rock musician. For one generation this may be Bob Dylan's "Like a Rolling Stone," while for another it could be Nirvana's "Smells Like Teen Spirit."

## » His Bag:

Kierkegaard is the winner in the "Who's-got-the-best-titles-for-their-philosophic-works" category: *Either/Or, Fear and Trembling, Sickness Unto Death*. He spent most of his time beating up on Hegel and his System, and is best known for pulling it all back to the individual with his declaration "Truth is subjectivity."

## » What's It to You:

Knowing that Kierkegaard is ground zero for existentialism will put you in the bonus round—he predates Sartre by nearly a century.

"Truth is subjectivity" wipes out the whole notion that Truth with a capital "T" exists. The concept is useful in delineating the lines of personal responsibility and serves as a solid underpinning for acts that may be considered of questionable morality. You might think of it as the philosophical/moral equivalent of Einstein's "It's all relative."

For example, your truth and the truth of the guy sitting across from you on the subway may be not only different but opposed, and that doesn't make either any less "true."

This is without a doubt one of the best possible ways to end any argument that appears to be in danger of derailing an evening. You and whomever you may be arguing with can both be right with a simple, "What was it Kierkegaard said, 'Truth is subjectivity'?"

## » His Bag #2:

Kierkegaard believed in a "lived" philosophy.

*Phase One*: Man starts out in Don Juan mode, drawn to Sensuality and reveling in wit—he is Aesthetic Man.

*Phase Two*: He then transitions into Socrates mode—journeying forth into the world of moral responsibility, and becomes Ethical Man.

*Phase Three*: At the end of his journey, realizing the futility of his quest for rationale, he takes the Leap of Faith, gunning for Eternity.

## » What's It to You:

Understand that even the greatest minds attempt to make sense of life by suggesting there is a path that can be followed. Understand that if your path vaguely approximates the above one, you might have a shot at enlightenment before you die.

# The Übermensch
# Friedrich Nietzsche 1844–1900

"*God is dead.*"                      —Friedrich Nietzsche

"*True Virtue is only for the aristocratic minority—a morality for all is ridiculous.*"      —Friedrich Nietzsche

"*Christianity was from the beginning, essentially and fundamentally, life's nausea and disgust with life, merely concealed behind, masked by, dressed up as, faith in 'another' or 'better' life.*" —Friedrich Nietzsche

## » His Bag:

The contribution for which Nietzsche will most be remembered: the *Übermensch* from *Thus Spake Zarathustra*. The *Übermensch* exercised his will to power in order to achieve an elevated, more powerful state of being, one beyond that of mere mortals. Nietzsche went on to say that the *Übermensch* need not be judged by the same standards as ordinary mortals, and that, if need be, he could engage in cruelty. (That's just one problem spot. Others include "the transvaluation of values" as well as some ideas about selective breeding, which led Hitler to find in Nietzsche the philosophical groundwork for Nazism. The linchpin to his thought lay in his conviction that morality of his day was rooted in social convention and things like the Bible—all of which were designed to drown out personal freedom. Were you to throw them away, you would be free.

## » What's It to You:

Understand that perversion of the "Will to Power," or sublimation of it, can change from being about achieving an elevated state into desiring to exert one's power over others. It is most useful when seeking to diffuse the "money is power" argument that many people in their late twenties and early thirties employ as their rationale for needing millions and millions of dollars.

"Look, you want the money and the power not for its own sake, but because you fell short in your quest for personal enlightenment."

## » His Bag #2:

Nietzsche had an elaborate system relating to Greek tragedy and the conflict between Apollo, symbol of order, form, and restraint, and Dionysus, the embodiment of passion and vital forces. He said it is the conflict between the two which generates Art. Moreover there was no Art in the nineteenth century because Christianity stifled everything. Nietzsche was down on Christianity, he wished to do away with the whole apparatus.

## » What's It to You:

Nietzsche's theorizing on Art predates Freud and shores up his historical standing. All claims to the contrary, Nietzsche was positively brilliant.

Personal Note: That Nietzsche's last days were spent in crazed fervor as syphilis ate large holes in his brain might help to explain the level of his delusions of grandiosity.

# William James (1842–1910)

*"Nothing is so fatiguing as the eternal hanging on of an uncompleted task."* —William James

*"A great many people think they are thinking when they are merely rearranging their prejudices."* —William James

*"The moral flabbiness born of the bitch-goddess* SUCCESS. *That—with the squalid cash interpretation put on the word success—is our national disease."* —William James

## » His Bag:

He helped make the Leap to Modernity with a focus on real-world application of philosophy. He also happens to be Henry James's big brother, which can put things in perspective when contemplating the whole sibling-rivalry thing. William James is one of the foremost American philosophers and a good psychologist to boot, but has been historically overshadowed by kid brother novelist.

James was a strong proponent of *Pragmatism*—truth is merely what's useful. He was interested in philosophy bettering people's lives as opposed to being an exercise in superpowered navel gazing.

## » What's It to You:

The whole concept of the bitch-goddess SUCCESS poised for a comeback in these economically motivated times.

*Option A*: Either admit to your worshiping at that altar: "I'm just one more acolyte chasing down the bitch-goddess SUCCESS," or

*Option B*: Show your moral fiber by dismissing the whole enterprise: "I know all about that bitch-goddess they call SUCCESS, and me, I want no part of it."

# Ludwig Wittgenstein (1889–1951)

"*Whereof one cannot speak, thereon one must
remain silent.*"                    —Ludwig Wittgenstein

» His Bag:

Wrote tricky-to-pronounce *Tractatus Logico-
Philosophicus*. Wittgenstein was firmly committed to
language, but found that language inherently was
extremely poor at expressing ineffable concepts like
"Truth"—the language we all use just isn't specific
enough. If you try to express such thoughts, you
produce linguistic nonsense.

» What's It to You:

Wittgenstein is the prince of the Put Your Money Where
Your Mouth Is School of Living. He gave away a sizable
inheritance after having a mystical experience at the
front in World War I, possibly while reading Tolstoy.

Moreover, in highly pensive moments when you are
being badgered relentlessly—"Jack, Jack, what is it? Jack,
why aren't you talking?"—it is reasonable to try out,
"What I'm experiencing right now, at this minute, I am
*incapable* of expressing *sufficiently*." And in so doing you
invoke Wittgenstein.

# Jean-Paul Sartre (1905–1980)

*"L'enfer, c'est les autres."* (*"Hell is other people."*)
—Jean-Paul Sartre

## » His Bag:

Existence precedes essence. You exist on the planet, and the task in your existence is to find out what the essence is. It is this quest that leads to a weird disjuncture that can be profoundly unsettling and that led Sartre to write books like *Nausea*. He was notoriously big on the "nothingness" of existence—there is no "there" there.

## » What's It to You:

As virtual life becomes more commonplace and we all fade into the computer screen, Sartre will become ever more relevant. The void between the individual and the world may only deepen as we recede into bits and bytes. In passing conversation suggest that you'd put your money on Sartre as the philosopher for the new millennium.

Either that or just throw off a "*Que sais-je?*" (Kuh-SAYJ) (*"What am I?"*) every once in a while.

# Cocktail Glasses and
# the Drinks That Go in Them

| GLASS | DRINKS | APPROPRIATE TIME TO ORDER |
|-------|--------|---------------------------|
| collins glass | Bloody Mary | Sunday Brunch—may be ordered at other times in case of extreme hangover |
| | Mint Julep | On the infield of the Kentucky Derby DURING the Kentucky Derby |
| highball glass | Long Island Iced Tea | In the summer daylight hours |
| | Cuba Libre | In extremely hot climates |
| | Vodka Tonic / Gin and Tonic | Anytime after noon—any day of the week |

| GLASS | DRINKS | APPROPRIATE TIME TO ORDER |
|---|---|---|
| cocktail glass/ martini glass  | Martini | In finer restaurants and bars. To be ordered with great discretion in all other environments |
| | Cosmopolitan | Under great duress or after having time-traveled to the 80s. |
| | Manhattan | In steak restaurants and hotel bars |
| old-fashioned | Black Russian | Sometime after 11 P.M.—preferably in Las Vegas, preferably up 500 dollars at a blackjack table |
| | Screwdriver | Breakfast, lunch, dinner, dancing |
| | Jack Daniel's (Rocks) | Wherever spirits are served |
| margarita glass | The Margarita | The blended slice of heaven—ordered only in summer or at your final office party at T.G.I.F. |

# MUSIC FOR THE MASSES

"Writing about Music is like dancing about Architecture."

—Anonymous

 *Visualize your path through a cocktail party as if it were a spring drive through the back roads of Vermont. Chatting over classic American Lit can be seen as the equivalent of bumping it up a notch as you see the 35 MPH signpost exiting town; riffing on the weekend's take at the box office is the two-lane straightaway where you ease up to ninety; and then there are all things musical: DANGER—SHARP TURN: SLOW TO 10 MPH. Music is just very personal, so proceed with caution, and know that everybody is entitled to their opinion.*

# Rock and Roll

Know the Faustian Bargain at the Center of Rock and Roll

Actually, it's at the center of the Blues, but Blues is at the center of Rock and Roll, so by extension . . .

As legend goes, a man (of the Blues) stands at the Crossroads of a deserted country road in the dark of a moonless night to wait for the Devil. The Devil arrives, and in trade for his immortal soul, the bluesman is granted a lifetime of easy living, bravura guitar playing, and women, women, women. The catch? Eternal damnation.

They say pioneering bluesman Robert Johnson (1911–1938) took that deal, and in his short twenty-seven years created music that could only come from the Devil, for as Johnson himself put it in song, "I got a hellhound on my trail."

The deal matches up neatly with the Live Fast, Die Hard ethos of Rock and Roll. The most prominent proponent of which, to this day, remains Led Zeppelin.[1]

---

1. Yes, Guns N' Roses partied hard. Yes, Van Halen pushed the envelope with the whole "We don't eat brown M & M's" bit, but really when it comes to the Faustian bargain of Rock and Roll, few can hold a candle to Led Zeppelin. They had their own jet, their own record label, their very own black-hearted patron saint in the form of Aleister Crowley, and did all manner of unspeakable things with people of questionable age.

# A Few Vague, General Statements about Rock and Roll to Get the Crowd Riled Up

## Rock Is Dead!²

This can also be framed as "Is Rock Dead?" but just get it out there. Evidence pointing to Rock's demise includes but is not limited to: the preponderance of knighthoods doled out to British rockers (Sir Phil Collins), the institutionalization of "Rock" as a backing track for capitalism (Elton John doing a Citibank commercial), and the possibility that guitar bands are simply no longer relevant.

The short version of the above: "Whatever energy rock had left after contending with Punk and New Wave has been completely run over by rap and hip-hop."

## Get with the Program and Talk about Digital Formats

Show your grasp of digital culture as you suggest with great enthusiasm that you look forward to the day when every song you ever wanted to hear will be accessible on the Internet *and* you'll be able to play it back on demand. Impress and befuddle your Luddite friends as you regale them with how you will be driving cross-country late on a Tuesday in spring 2003 and, suddenly seized by a desire to hear Meat Loaf's "Paradise by the

---

2. Rock Is Dead closely parallels another great canon-buster posited by Friedrich Nietzsche, "God is dead." Rock Stars are hailed as gods, and the excesses of the genre, with its attendant arena shows, private jets, and rituals such as burning a lighter for an encore, are at least as complicated as those of any other organized religion and are, if not passé, at the very least tired.

Dashboard Light," you dial a code into your car radio and within seconds be blessed with:

"Do you love me?
Do you love me forever . . ."

---

» *Best Movie Scene Dealing
  with Digital Format Issues*

*When you mention format and someone says Huh? try the following:* "Remember that scene in Men in Black *where Tommy Lee Jones grabs the little white disc, y'know, he and Will Smith are hanging out in the MIB lab and Tommy Lee is showing off all the great benefits of alien technology and he grabs this tiny little thing, like a mini-mini-mini CD, and says,* "Guess I'll have to buy the White Album *again"? That's a format issue.*

---

## Beatles or Stones?[3]

Got to have an answer. Wouldn't be prudent not to. The Beatles and the Rolling Stones are *the* Rock and Roll archetypes.[4] Everything the Stones did, save getting busted for recreational drug usage, the Beatles did first. And in this era of *first-mover advantage*, that makes the Beatles the biggest band ever.

---

3. There is the option of answering Beatles *vs.* Stones with "the Kinks." It's appropriately left-field—correct time frame, easier to bluff—and just knowing the Kinks can breathe the same air as these icons is a good starting place. Should backup ammunition be required, rifle off in quick succession "Lola" (best song ever about cross-dressing), "You Really Got Me," "All Day and All the Night," and finish with the poetic majesty of "Celluloid Heroes" as a kicker.
   "I wish my life was a non-stop Hollywood movie show
   A fantasy world of celluloid villains and heroes."
4. The British rock band Oasis did, however, for a period in the mid-1990s, attempt to have their cake and eat it too, ripping off the Beatles' sound and behaving like the Rolling Stones—models, drugs, public brawls.

|  | THE BEATLES | THE ROLLING STONES |
|---|---|---|
| First Album | *Please, Please Me,* March 22, 1963 | *The Rolling Stones,* May 29, 1964 |
| First Ed Sullivan Appearance | February 9, 1964 | October 25, 1964 |
| First Movie | *Help,* 1964 | *Sympathy for the Devil,* 1968 |
| First Weird Drug-Induced Psychedelic Album | *Sgt. Pepper's Lonely Hearts Club Band,* June 1, 1967 | *Their Satanic Majesties Request* November 27, 1967 |
| Breakup | 1970 | How much money does one group of people need? |
| Induction into Rock Hall of Fame | 1988 | 1989 |

## Of Course Elvis Is King, and No, 30 Million Elvis Fans Can't Be Wrong

Suggest that Elvis is a lot like Augustine's concept of God,[5] existing outside of Space and Time. Much of the basics of Elvisology[6] are widespread, so show that you know the granular, personal side, because even if you aren't down with the King, it's part of being alive to know something beyond "Elvis has left the building. . . ."

---

5. See "Philosophy for Philistines."
6. *Elvisology* is the official term for "historical and statistical information concerning the life and career of Elvis Presley," as ordained by the estate of Elvis Presley.

- TCB: Elvis's motto—"Takin' Care of Business" (in a flash). In the modern vernacular it is the appropriate response to:

  "Whatcha doin', Johnny?"

  "TCB, Mabel, TCB."

  (Memphis accents are optional.)

- It's been said before. He died on the john.
- Refer to the two-part chronicle of the King's life by the author Peter Guralnick, *Last Train to Memphis: The Rise of Elvis Presley* and *Careless Love: The Unmaking of Elvis Presley,* as the finest example of Rock and Roll biography.[7]
- Challenge your company to come up with a meeting more full of irony, humor, pathos, and satire than when Elvis Presley in full seventies regalia—jumpsuit, sideburns, sunglasses and chains—met the then President of the United States, Richard Milhous Nixon, to show his support in the war on drugs.

## Make Really Grandiose Statements about Tectonic Shifts in the Pop Music Marketplace

» Grandiose Statement #1:"Punk and New Wave, in their reaction to the excesses of Arena Rock, are similar to Marx and Kierkegaard in their reaction to Hegel."

Hegel, in the late nineteenth century, had become the entrenched philosophical norm;[8] his system of logic was

---

7. Other hallowed Rock and Roll biographies include but are not limited to: Led Zeppelin—*Hammer of the Gods*; Bob Marley—*Catch a Fire*; and Jim Morrison—*No One Here Gets Out Alive.*

8. Again, see "Philosophy for Philistines" to see what the man who coined the term *Zeitgeist* was really all about.

so much a part of university and intellectual life that it had, in effect, become flaccid.

Rock and Roll in the mid-seventies had become the entrenched musical norm, so incredibly bland, so mindlessly banal—the Eagles flourished—that it had, in effect, become flaccid. Punk and New Wave, with equal but different energies, tore the monster Rock edifice asunder.

## Remind Everybody That Fashion Has Always Been a Large Part of Rock and Roll

» Grandiose Statement #2: "Punk rock was more about fashion than it was about anarchy."

Rock and Roll purists will insist it's about more than the clothes. The Sex Pistols were a kind of turning point in the history of Rock and Roll, but they began as little more than the marketing brainchild of a Machiavellian entrepreneur by the name of Malcom McLaren. The band wore all those safety pins and ripped jeans not as a show of defiance or rebellion but rather to help McLaren move merchandise out of the shop he shared with his designer friend, Vivienne Westwood. That whole bit about the Pistols changing the face of Rock and Roll irrevocably—that came later.

» Grandiose Statement #3: "David Bowie and Madonna have had remarkably similar trajectories."

Who can change more in the history of their career, the Material Girl or the Man Who Sold the World?

| | DAVID BOWIE | MADONNA |
|---|---|---|
| Phase One<br>The Arrival | Folk Rock with a Twist<br>—*Hunky Dory* | Dance Club Diva—<br>"Get Into the Groove" |
| Phase Two<br>Making the<br>Name | *Ziggy Stardust, Aladdin Sane*, Front Man<br>for Glam Rock | "Boy-Toy" *Like a Virgin*—<br>Nation of Madonna<br>Wannabes |
| Phase Three<br>Refining the Act | "The Thin White Duke" | "Material Girl" |
| Phase Four<br>Shaking Up the Act | *Berlin Trilogy*<br>with Brian Eno | *Sex, Erotica* |
| Phase Five<br>Taking a Detour That<br>Surprises Everybody | *The Tin Machine* | *Evita*—"Don't Cry<br>for Me, Argentina" |
| Phase Six<br>Come Into Your Own<br>on Your Own Terms | Internet Guy—Launch<br>davidbowie.com<br>Sell yourself on the<br>Bond Market | New-Age-Spouting<br>Yoga-Doing<br>Cabala-Following<br>"Ray of Light" |
| Phase Seven<br>International<br>Fashion Icon | Mix film career with<br>family life, budding<br>businesses, and art | Mix film career with<br>family life, budding<br>businesses, and yoga |

## Be Passionate about Liner Notes

Caring about minutiae such as liner notes is a sure sign of world-class devotee-ism. Lament that CDs have made the art of the liner note a more rare and splendid thing. Reference the brilliant liner notes written by director/journalist Cameron Crowe for Bob Dylan's *Biograph*.

And to amuse and entertain your literary friends, recall that Thomas Pynchon, a novelist accustomed to taking well over 1 million words to get his point across, penned liner notes for a then unheard-of band called Lotion.[9]

## Vague but Important Job 2007b: Record Producer

It's always valuable to have a dream job floating around in the back of your mind, like overseeing all of the Condé Nast magazines or designing the sets for the MTV Beach Houses around the world. Into that category might fall Star Record Producer, for which there is no real job description aside from being able to help a band hone its "style."

Specifically, if you were to spend time dreaming about which producer you might want to be, two suggestions that spring to mind are Rick Rubin and Daniel Lanois. You might want to be the former because he was behind Run-DMC, the Beastie Boys, the Red Hot Chili

---

9. The notes accompanied the 1996 album called *Nobody's Cool.* And Mr. Pynchon's parting words were, "Find the remote, get out the Snapple and Cheetos and like the Love Boat staff always sez, 'welcome aboard.'"

Peppers, Public Enemy, and a minor renaissance from Johnny Cash.

And you might want to be the latter because there are fewer all-around weirdo-cool guys with the "unlimited-respect-for-reasons-that-can't-be-articulated" than Daniel Lanois. And you could get away with doing things like bringing an entire full-size circus tent inside your house in order to "create a vibe," which is what he did when he produced Luscious Jackson's *Fever In, Fever Out*.

Challenge anyone to come up with a more complete re-invention of a band's sound than U2's *Achtung Baby*. The Provider: Daniel Lanois.

## Five Schools of Rap and Their Leaders

Even if the best you can do is manage a weak smile and say, "Jiggy with it?" here's some background on the Rap revolution.

| STYLE | BANDS | TRACKS YOU CAN REMEMBER | GENERAL MESSAGE |
|---|---|---|---|
| Old School (1979–1985) | Sugarhill Gang Grandmaster Flash and the Furious Five | "Rapper's Delight" "White Lines" "The Message" | Party down. |
| East Coast Rap (1982–?) | Run-DMC | "My Adidas" | Hey, you can make a whole Rap album! |

MU/IC

| STYLE | BANDS | TRACKS YOU CAN REMEMBER | GENERAL MESSAGE |
|---|---|---|---|
| Hardcore Rap (1984–?) | Public Enemy | "Don't Believe the Hype" | This shit is political. |
| Gangsta Rap (1986–?) | N.W.A. | "Straight Outta Compton" | Ghetto life makes for good storytelling. |
| Afrocentrics/ Native Tongue (1989–?) | De La Soul Tribe Called Quest | "Me Myself and I" "I Left My Wallet in El Segundo"[10] | Mama Afrikaa |

## » The Great Crossover

*Rap entered the mainstream when Run-DMC mixed it up with Aerosmith[11] for a reissue of "Walk This Way." The rock-guitar riff mixed with the beats of Rap proved to be the perfect recipe for the Great Crossover.*

---

10. "I left my wallet in El Segundo" remains a cultural touchstone that managed to permeate the national subconscious. For years people have reached for their back pocket and begun, "I left my wallet . . ." and then, as if in surprise, finished to themselves, ". . . in El Segundo."
11. The byproduct of this, of course, was the resurgence of Aerosmith the band, a wholly unnecessary occurrence, though there was a brief moment in the 1980s when they did contribute positively to society and culture with a trio of videos introducing the then cherubic Alicia Silverstone.

81

# Rock and Roll Death: A Primer

Death traditionally enters into most conversations about Rock and Roll in either the eighth, seventeenth, or thirty-seventh minute, from "The Day the Music Died" to Kurt Cobain sticking a shotgun in his mouth.[12]

## Once and for All: The Day the Music Died

Decoding the cryptic and wistful "American Pie" by Don McLean was, for a brief period, a national pastime. Using as its starting point the February 1959 plane crash that took the lives of Ritchie "La Bamba" Valens, Buddy Holly, and the Big Bopper, the song lays out a sentimental overview of Rock and Roll and the turbulent times that shaped it.[13]

With a total running time of eight and a half minutes, to detail each and every reference would put you in

---

12. "Did she or didn't she?" as in "Did Courtney Love help or at the very least not prevent the death of Kurt Cobain," is one of the more lasting Rock and Roll mysteries. You can always reference the documentary by Nick Broomfield—which never quite says "She did," but it doesn't really leave much room for doubt. To prove you've seen the film, you can and should mention the hilarious and depressing nature of Courtney's former friends in Seattle and the climactic scene wherein Broomfield confronts Love while she is accepting a humanitarian award for advancing the right of free speech. The irony being that Love sought to suppress Broomfield's film as slander and would not allow him to use any of Cobain's music.
13. Roberta Flack was so inspired by the song that she wrote her extremely sad and powerful "Killing Me Softly." This was later covered by the Fugees. (File this one under funny generational shit.)

league with conspiracy theorists who tie John F. Kennedy's assassination to the Great Schism,[14] and for copyright reasons we can't publish all the lyrics. But we can offer the one key reference that might never have made sense: "Drove my Chevy to the Levee but the Levee was dry. . . ."

Well, that little line refers to three college students who were killed during the summer of '64 for trying to help get out the black vote in Mississippi[15]—their bodies were found in a levee.

## Be Able to Use "Death by Misadventure" in a Sentence

Leave it to a British coroner to turn a phrase. Rolling Stones guitarist Brian Jones was found floating facedown in his swimming pool on July 3, 1969. The coroner's report featured the choice turn of phrase "death by mis-adventure" due to "immersion in fresh water under the influence of drugs and alcohol." Feel free to appropriate this phrase as you see fit, in relation to activities such as swimming, driving, or sledding in a state of intoxication, i.e., "You wouldn't want to suffer death by misadventure, now would you?"

---

14. The Great Schism: When the popes were split between Rome and Avignon. A great historical moment that should be referenced whenever possible. It's historical, has gravitas, and makes it seem like you know your history (Church History, even).
15. Adding to your already vast pop-culture knowledge, throw in that this incident, in case anyone forgot, was also the subject matter of a film by Alan Parker titled *Mississippi Burning*.

## And in the Category of Unsung Rock Deaths

A run-down Brit named Stiv Bators,[16] who can be seen either as a second-rate Iggy Pop or a better-behaved Sid Vicious, depending on which icon you most venerate, expired in the following fashion. Mr. Bators had retired to Paris to "work some stuff out." One day while crossing the street, Stiv was struck by a van. He then dusted himself off and wandered home.

Two days later he was found dead of internal injuries. As the story goes, Stiv was so completely out of it, so absolutely gone, that he did not realize the extent of his injuries. So when Celebrity Death is the topic, hold back your Bators anecdote until the last. And don't forget to mention that one of his earlier incarnations was as the leader of a band named the Dead Boys.

## How to Make a Few Seminal Guilty Pleasures Understandable to Others

We all have a CD or twenty-five hiding out underneath all the rest; maybe it's the first Wham! ("Wake Me Up before You Go-Go") single or the dance-mix versions of Diana Ross's greatest hits (seventeen minutes of "Love Hangover"). Regardless, they're there and they're not going away. And with the proper amount of self-deprecation and context, there are ways to share these hidden chestnuts. A few examples:

---

16. Aside from this ignominious death, Mr. Bators might also be remembered for his role in the scratch-and-sniff classic from John Waters, *Polyester*.

## Show How Your Guilty Pleasure Fits into a Continuum of Western Thought: Barry White

When Barry White sings "You're my first, my last, my everything. . . ." it's his good lovin' way of saying that somebody is the alpha and the omega[17]—the sum total of all. Admitting openly a certain love of Barry White shows that you are brave, secure, and know the meaning of the term "boudoir," and combining that with a classical Greek reference should shelter you from any mean-spirited anti "Voice of Love" harm.

## Know Hidden Gems in Your Guilty Pleasure's Catalog: Neil Diamond

While it is possible that few could take issue with Neil Diamond, a man who has sung the likes of "Sweet Caroline," "Cracklin' Rosie," and "I Am . . . I Said," not to mention having supplied the sound track for *E.T.* (*Heartlight*). There are those who might think Neil is too over the top. To the naysayers, you can do one of two things: Point to the highlight of his career, the sound track for the film version of "Jonathan Livingston Seagull"; or ask if they have ever heard "The Pot-Smoker's Song" on *Velvet Gloves and Spit.* The anti-drug ditty features spoken word outtakes of real-life pot-smokers, was way ahead of its time (1968), and would make even the most jaded hard-core musical snob sit back and smile.

---

17. Alpha being the first letter of the Greek alphabet, omega the last.

## Just Admit that Every Once in a While It's Important for You to Feel Twelve: Cheap Trick *Live at Budokan*

There's no shame in admitting that you, like Tom Cruise in *Risky Business*, occasionally like to run around in your skivvies and just rock out. Just don't admit to the wearing-the-sunglasses-inside-the-house bit.

Other groups and songs that fall squarely into this category:

> Boston: "More Than a Feeling"
>
> Bob Seger and the Silver Bullet Band: "Night Moves"
>
> The Steve Miller Band: "Swing Town"

## A Game: Memories

When things slow, attempt the following: Name three songs from your past (or present) that specifically recall a significant moment in time. And tell why. A pool from which you can choose if things do not immediately come to mind:

> "Roadhouse Blues," The Doors
> For that fraternity-boy nihilism you claim to have once experienced. "I woke up this morning and I got myself a beer. . . ."
>
> "Black Coffee in Bed" and "Pulling Mussels from a Shell," Squeeze
> If you attended college at any point from 1980 to 1990, this should take you back.
>
> "Call Me" and "Heart of Glass," Blondie
> "Call Me" for its thundering rhythms and the vague memory of Richard Gere hanging upside down doing upside-down

pull-ups with gravity boots in the eighties masterpiece *American Gigolo*. "Heart of Glass" for getting everyone out on the dance floor, no matter where you are, no matter what time it is, and regardless of what the boy-girl ratio happens to be.

"Rock Lobster," The B-52s
Well, duh.

"It's Raining Men," The Weathergirls
Because there is nothing in this world like watching a dance club full of gay men burst with joy when this song comes on. "Hallelujah, It's Raining Men!"

# Jazz

When it comes to jazz, you've got your aficionados— the guys who know every single note of every single performance of "Koko"[18] by Charlie Parker and what that note . . . *there* . . . means to the history of mankind. And then there's everybody else. This section is for everybody else.

## Know Why Jazz Is the Greatest American Art Form

Because a wise man once said so. Actually the wise man, who happens to be my friend Bob, said, "Jazz is the greatest American art form because it is the discipline of

---

18. "Koko" is a tune developed by Parker that is generally considered to mark the beginning of "Bop." The phenomenal speed of his playing; the phrasing at odd lengths of three, five, and seven bars, as opposed to two, four, and eight; and the wildly innovative lines that would swirl outside of the main line were the earmarks of this signature tune.

classical combined with the improvisational techniques of the natural musician." And he's right.

## Know the Evolution

Fractional elements exist all along the fringes, but the chronology looks something like this:

| GENRE | MAJOR FIGURE(S) | SEMINAL RECORDING | BEST LISTENING ENVIRONMENT/ SOUNDS LIKE |
|---|---|---|---|
| Traditional Jazz | Louis Armstrong | Hot Fives Hot Sevens | The beginning of a Woody Allen film. The music you hear in your head when you are reading *The Great Gatsby* |
| Big Band/ Swing | Benny Goodman | *Benny Goodman Carnegie Hall Jazz Concert* | A really good old-school wedding |
| Bebop The Forties | Charlie Parker (Alto Sax) Dizzy Gillespie (Trumpet) Thelonious Monk (pianist) | *Jazz at Massey Hall* *Night in Tunisia* *Straight, No Chaser* | Late-night bar with two packs of cigarettes in front of you, a shot of whiskey in your glass, and boundless enthusiasm to keep up with the players onstage |

| GENRE | MAJOR FIGURE(S) | SEMINAL RECORDING | BEST LISTENING ENVIRONMENT/ SOUNDS LIKE |
|---|---|---|---|
| Cool The Fifties | Miles Davis | *Kind of Blue* | Sunday mornings with the *New York Times* and a crisp fall day |
| Free Jazz Late Sixties | Ornette Coleman John Coltrane | *Free Jazz* *A Love Supreme* | Entering the Metropolitan Museum of Art for a cocktail party |

## Show Your Musical History by Affirming That You Know Your Satchmo

> "*Louis Armstrong's station in the history of jazz is unimpeachable. If it weren't for him, there wouldn't be any of us.*"
> —Dizzy Gillespie, 1971

**Opinion:**

If you take Louis Armstrong and Duke Ellington and put them together, you've got most of early-twentieth-century music.

When you talk about Louis, born in New Orleans in 1901, the key words are phrasing and intonation. The man had a gift for melody. You can throw around the notion that Louis is the first jazz genius. He transformed jazz from an ensemble form to a soloist showcase, and he invented that scat-singing stuff.

## Be Able to Give a Quick (and I Do Mean Quick) Sax History Lesson Featuring Lester Young, Charlie "Yardbird" Parker, and John "Trane" Coltrane

"Okay. You want to know the brief history of Jazz saxophone? Here goes: First there was Lester Young. And he was good. Then there was Charlie Parker, and he took what Lester Young did and he played it 'twice as fast.' Then Trane took what Bird did and he played *it* 'twice as fast.' There you go from Swing to Bop to Free Jazz, thank you very much."

## How to Express the Undeniable Virtuosity That Was and Is Charlie Parker: You Don't

The only thing written about more often than Parker playing sax is how impossible it was to write about Parker playing sax. But as an illustration of his talent, relate the following anecdote. You could call it "If Only I Had a Better Axe."[19]

It's May 1953. Parker's on the lam . He's got a show to play in Toronto with Dizzy Gillespie, Charles Mingus, Max Roach, and Bud Powell. And Parker, he doesn't even have his horn. As the story goes, he sold it before the show to get some smack. And they're looking everywhere to find the guy a horn. They can't find him one, but they've got all this talent together and they really want Bird to play. So they find him a toy plastic saxophone, like the kind a six-year-old monkeys around with

---

19. Axe is a common term for both the saxophone and the guitar. It is that thing that musicians play. Use with extreme caution.

after his birthday party! And Parker makes that toy sax howl—blowing nothing but discordant, beautiful note after discordant, beautiful note. (And he's credited as Charlie Chan to boot to avoid a squabble with his record company.)

## Some Facts about Miles Davis

Everyone knows Miles Davis. Miles Davis is to Jazz what Picasso is to Art. Prolific, trend-setting, monolithic, misunderstood, misanthropic, misogynistic, and uniquely Miles.

> Miles Davis was a motherfucker.[20]

> Miles Davis was married to Cicely Tyson.

> Miles Davis holed himself in his house for seven years doing "blow and whores" until Cicely came and said, "Miles, enough."

> Miles Davis enjoyed playing with his back to the audience.

> Miles Davis enjoyed using the word "nigger" and he enjoyed talking about his distrust and loathing for white people.

> Miles Davis lost control of his Lamborghini and shattered both of his ankles.

> In an interview wherein Miles Davis is asked about some unpleasant things he wrote in his *auto*biography he replies, "I haven't got there yet."

---

20. Motherfucker being the highest possible compliment that one can pay to a certain kind of jazz musician. As in, "That guy. That guy is a motherfucker!" said with great enthusiasm.

## To Play Like the Bird, You Got to Be Like the Bird

Charlie Parker was an alcoholic, a junkie, and a woman-izer, and he had a propensity for fried chicken. (On occasion he was known to indulge in all three at the same time, as described in Miles Davis's autobiography, *Miles.*) The one thing he did a lot of, aside from playing sax, was shooting heroin.

Parker was an absolute wash-out as a role model as "To play like the Bird, you got to be like the Bird" was a kind of mantra/rationalization for youngsters coming up the ranks who would shoot up in an effort to achieve some of that Bird-like inspiration.

**Cheese Points:**

Upon examining Charlie Parker's corpse, the coroner estimated him to be fifty-five years old. He had just turned thirty-five.

## Ornette Coleman and Free Jazz

If you want people to think you're intense, say you really like to listen to Ornette Coleman. Coleman plays some of the most out-of-sync, off-key, wacky music known to man. Think of Ornette Coleman as being to jazz what Jackson Pollock was to painting, William Faulkner was to literature, and Frank Gehry is to architecture. Innovative, incomprehensible, and hailed as a genius.

You can back up that he's a genius by pointing to his being named a MacArthur Fellow[21] in July 1994.

---

21. MacArthur Fellows receive upwards of $300,000 over a five-year period—no strings attached. It has come to be known as the "genius" grant and is funded by the John D. and Catherine T. MacArthur Foundation.

# Opera

## What People Talk About

Opera is a fetishist's paradise: the costumes, the staging, the voices, the interpretations, the story, the song. The basics are the Germans and the Italians, and the French had *Carmen*, but that's an advanced course. Here's the short sheet for the major showstoppers.

## It's All about How You Say It

As so much of it is about language, pronunciation is the key. A few examples:

> Richard Wagner—It's VAHG-ner.
> It's not pretentious. It's the way it's said.

> Richard Strauss—It's RIK-ard Shtrauss.

> Bayreuth—In this German town Wagner erected a theater in which to perform his complex operas. It is pronounced Buy-ROYT, not Bay-ROOT. That's another place altogether.

> Cecilia Bartoli—Che-CHEEL-ya Bar-TOH-lee.
> The leading mezzo-soprano of the day.

# The Italians

## Gioacchino Antonio Rossini (1792–1868)

> *Opera: The Barber of Seville*
> *Written:* 1816
> *Setting:* Seville, Spain (eighteenth century)
> *The Story:* Figaro, the Barber in *Barber of Seville,* is

enlisted to help Count Almaviva in his pursuit of Rosina, ward of Dr. Bartolo. Bartolo, however, has other plans. Figaro saves the day; the Count, who needs to disguise himself twice in order to do so, gets the girl; and the romp ends happily ever after.

*The Comment on the Music:* "Dig the vocal pyrotechnics; Rossini likes to make his people work."

*The Comment on the Show:* "Now tell me, who would have been fooled by those disguises?"

## Giuseppe Verdi (1813–1901)

*The Operas: La Traviata, Rigoletto, Aida*
(also *Il Trovatore*)
*Opening Gambit:* "When it comes to Verdi, like Mozart, I have such a hard time deciding which one is my favorite."

### » Rigoletto

*Written:* 1851
*Setting:* Court of the Duke of Mantua
*The Story:* Based on Victor Hugo's play *Le Roi s'Amuse* about a hunchbacked jester by the name of Rigoletto. The aforementioned Duke chases after Rigoletto's daughter Gilda. The displeased hunchback hires a hitman, who misses his mark, taking out Gilda instead.

*The Comment on the Performance:* "Again with the hunchbacks? What's up with Victor Hugo anyway?"

### » La Traviata

*Written:* 1853
*Setting:* Paris
*The Story:* Rich boy falls for girl from the wrong side

of the tracks. Aristocratic Alfredo gets himself all tied up in knots over Violetta, a prostitute on death's door. Dad convinces him it's not worth it, but as Violetta lies dying, Dad consents for one long, heart-wrenching good bye.

*The Jury Is Still Out:* Try to figure out where your company stands: Was it the Maria Callas performance or that of Dame Joan Sutherland that should be considered the standard?

*About the Music:* "I've always maintained it's the pathos within the music that makes the opera, but that 'bel canto'[22] stuff wears a fellow down."

*About the Performance:* "Is it my imagination or was she dying *the whole entire time?*"

*If you had to explain it to somebody at gunpoint:* Think *Pretty Woman* but Julia Roberts has TB and Richard Gere is running his father's company, as opposed to his own.

## » Aida

*Written:* 1871

*Setting:* Ancient Egypt—Egypt and Ethiopia are at war.

*The Story:* Love and War amongst the pyramids. Aida, daughter of Amonasro (King of Ethiopia), falls for Radames, leader of the Egyptian army, which doesn't sit well with Princess Amneris, who has had her eyes on Radames for some time. Radames captures Amonasro. Dad gets daughter to dupe her lover Radames into giving up precious military secrets. Amneris tells everybody about it. Radames is sentenced to die alone, buried alive in a pyramid. Aida sneaks in, they spend their dying moments together, and Amneris is left distraught and alone.

---

22. Bel canto literally means "beautiful singing."

*In Toto:* "A little overblown for my tastes—the full-scale pyramid always seems out of place—but that last scene when she sneaks in to die by his side wipes me out every time."

## Giacomo Puccini (1858–1924)

*The Operas: Tosca, La Bohème*
*(also Madame Butterfly)*

### » La Bohème

*Written:* 1896. Based on the H. Murger novel
*La Vie de Bohème,* 1848.

*Setting:* 1830, Paris

*The Story:* Seamstress Mimi and poet Rodolfo meet in a freezing garret in Paris. They fall in love. He gets jealous and she leaves. They're reunited tragically as she is dying.

*What You Can Say:* Talk about how it's not so much about the characters but about the bohemian life. E.g.:

"Once I started to get into it for the mood, the bohemian feel, instead of the characters, I found I liked it so much more."

### » Tosca

*Written:* 1900

*Setting:* Rome, 1800

*The Story:* Let's get sordid with a nice little turn-of-the-century political love triangle. Scarpia, the mean-spirited chief of police, and Cavaradossi, a republican and an artist, are both in love with Tosca, the star soprano of the Roman opera. Scarpia tortures Cavaradossi until Tosca agrees to let him have his way (and give away a few of Cavaradossi's political secrets). Thinking freedom is just around the corner for her and her lover, she stabs Scarpia. But it's too late; Cavaradossi has been taken out by the Secret Police. A defeated Tosca hurls herself from the Castel San Angelo.

*The Good Word:* Scarpia is one of the better villains in all of opera and Tosca one of the most lovable. Declare, "I don't care if the story line reads like a nighttime soap; I still love it."

## The Germans

### Wolfgang Amadeus Mozart (1756–1791)

*Le Nozze di Figaro, Don Giovanni (also Cosi Fan Tutte)*— all three done with the librettist Lorenzo da Ponte.

#### » Le Nozze di Figaro

*Written:* 1785

*Setting:* Seville, Spain

*Story:* Figaro (a valet) and Susanna (a maid) are getting married. The Count has the right, but not the obligation, to sleep with Susanna (*droit du seigneur*).[23] He gives up this right and then tries to trick her into bed anyway.

*The Good Word:* "Sure, it's the pinnacle of *Opera Buffa,* but there's enough nudge-nudge wink-wink in there for the entire run of *Three's Company.*"

---

23. French phrase for the right of the master to sleep with those in his keep or stead.

## » Don Giovanni

*Written:* 1787

*Story:* An unrepentant Don Juan, Don Giovanni takes whomever he wants whenever he wants her. And so far that has equaled in Italy, 640; in Germany, 231; in France, 100; in Turkey, 91; and in Spain, 1,003. (These numbers come courtesy of manservant Leporello.) D.G. meets his end when the statue of the commendatore comes to life and drags him unrepentant down to hell.

*The Good Word:* Refer to *Don Giovanni* as the most perfect opera. It's got everything it should have. The music is genius, the structure is superb. It has every single element a great opera should.

### Know the Dish on the Diva

Maria Callas, or Callas (she is usually referred to simply by her last name, often accompanied by a deep anguished sigh in recognition of her greatness), is not considered so much for her voice, which was indeed a fine one, but more for the drama she infused into her performances. There have been greater voices, but not greater performers. (She also was famously thrown over by Aristotle Onassis when Jackie Kennedy arrived on the scene.)

## And Now a Moment of Silence for John Cage

Be amused at the American composer's masterwork, *4' 33".* A pianist arrives at a piano, sits there for four minutes and thirty-three seconds without playing one note . . . and then leaves.

# LINGUISTIC INTERLUDE II: GERMAN

*German, not Italian, is the official language of Art History. In a random survey of 3,400 hungover students between the ages of 19 and 27, German was a close second to Chinese in languages a person least wants to hear at a high volume and at an early hour.*

*Here are some German terms that add a certain dramatic and worldly quality to everyday speech.*

»*Doppelgänger* (DOP-pul-GENG-er)

Your double—either fictional or real. If you, while out on the town, see somebody who looks like a friend of yours, you might say, "My God, Ian, I saw your Doppelgänger last night."

If you are blamed for an act that is uncharitable and for which you do not wish to accept responsibility: "That wasn't me, that was my Doppelgänger."

»*Schadenfreude* (SHAH-den-FROY-duh)

When you feel good about something bad happening to somebody you know. Not to be admitted in public but good to accuse others of experiencing. When your good friend's good friend has his net worth halved by a precipitous dip in the stock market, you can suggest, "Come on, you felt a little bit of Schadenfreude—admit it."

»*Sturm und Drang* (SHTURM-unt-DRAHNG)

A really heavyhanded way of referring to melodrama, personal or otherwise. Best used in a third-person context referring to somebody who enjoys a certain level of soap-opera histrionics in his life. "Oh, you know Xavier, he just loves the Sturm und Drang of it all."

»*Wunderkind* (VOON-der-kint)

The word du jour for the Internet whiz kids. Wildly bright, talented beyond their years, and, at the end of the century, wealthy beyond their wildest dreams.

# The Dynamic Nature of Acoustics at a Cocktail Party

### The Scenario:

You are stranded with a complete stranger at a cocktail party with no possible exit.

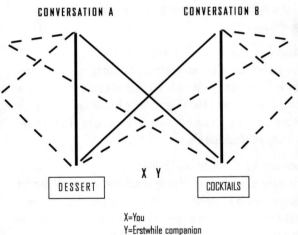

CONVERSATION A          CONVERSATION B

DESSERT          X   Y          COCKTAILS

X=You
Y=Erstwhile companion
 aka total stranger

The Solution:

Expound on the dynamic nature of acoustics within the cocktail party environment. By identifying two sources equidistant from central locations you can effectively filter out background noise and hear what somebody is saying from across the room.

How To:

1. Choose two conversations as shown—
   Conversation A and Conversation B.

2. Draw your erstwhile companion's attention to Conversations A and B.

3. Gesturing scientifically with your index finger, draw the paths that the conversations A and B can travel, either directly, as indicated by the solid lines, or indirectly, as seen by the dotted lines. (Make reference to how the trajectory of these dotted lines is much like a cue ball bouncing off the cushion of a billiard table.)

4. Explain that if Person Y so desired they could hear Conversation A and/or B by simply doing the following.

   A. Identify voices in Conversation A.

   B. Identify voices in Conversation B.

   C. Focus on *hearing* Conversation A at the same time as *filtering* Conversation B.

5. Witness their amazement and glee at now being able to eavesdrop successfully throughout the party. Suggest they might try to see if it works elsewhere in the room.

*From "Blind Source Separation"—an experiment undertaken at the Interval Research Corporation by Tom Ngo and Neal Badkamkar.*

# LITERATURE FOR THE LAZY

"I haven't read the book. . . . You don't need to read the book to have an opinion on it. I prefer good literary criticism, that way you get the novelist's ideas as well as the critic's thinking."

—Tom Townsend (Edward Clements I)

in the film *Metropolitan*

## Strike a Pose

Talking about books can, if you so desire, be as easy
as flipping through the daily paper or checking your
e-mail. Take one part attitude, one part knowledge, and
throw a smidge of literary criticism into the mix, and
you have the makings of a passable critical voice.
However, on the off chance that you can't find it within
yourself to muster the "one part knowledge," forthwith
are some ploys that might contribute to your appearing
well read.

## Love Your Greeks—Namely Homer

Eighth century B.C.: The *Iliad* and the *Odyssey* are the
starting points of Western Literature, and having some
knowledge of the stories and their author is a necessity.

### The Respective Stories

The *Iliad*: It's the last year of the Trojan War, and
Achilles, like an athlete with a bad hamstring, is sitting
on the sidelines. When his good friend Patroclus is taken
out by the Trojan warrior Hector, Achilles joins the fray.
Achilles wins the day and in a grand and tragic gesture
hands the Trojan king Priam the body of Priam's own
son, Hector.

The *Odyssey*: The story of the hero Odysseus' ten-
year journey to rejoin his wife, Penelope, following the
Trojan War.

## How to Mine the Pretension of the Oral Tradition

Both the *Iliad* and the *Odyssey* are meant to be read aloud and cited as verse, as opposed to being read as prose. This affords one the opportunity to throw out not just one but two pretentious statements.

» **Pretentious Statement #1:**

"You know, when I read the *Iliad* or the *Odyssey*, I just have to read it aloud, as if to an audience."

» **Pretentious Statement #2:**

"You know what I've always wanted? To really understand what Homer was going for in his original tongue, y'know? 'Tell me, O muse, of that ingenious hero who traveled far and—' Sure, it's epic stuff, even in English, but in the Greek, in the Greek, it would be sublime."

## Quote from Homer as if He Is the Ultimate Advice Columnist

Dropping Homeric references in casual conversation[1] suggests a deep understanding of the poet's oeuvre, and a familiarity with "the Classics."

» **On Dangerous Women**

*The Idea to Present*
"Beware the Siren song."
    *The Meaning:* A woman who is alluring, tempting,

---

1. See "Mythology for the Mainstream," pp. 24–26, for more information of this variety.

gorgeous, and nothing but trouble is a siren. With heads of females and bodies of birds—the Sirens (from the *Odyssey*)—sang songs so sweet that sailors would steer their boats off-course to glimpse them and, in so doing, crash. See also women who wear hats, leather pants, and have great facility with the phrase "Baby."

## » On How to Stay Out of Trouble

*The Idea to Present*
"Lash yourself to the mast."

*The Meaning:* Odysseus, in order not to fall prey to the Siren song, had his men lash him to the mast. In so doing he became the first mortal to escape their singing.

## Fake Knowing a Lot by Knowing Very Little

### Have Passing Knowledge of at Least One Really Large Unyielding Work—if Not Two

Works that qualify as "really large and unyielding" include, but are not limited to, Virgil's *Aeneid*, Dante Alighieri's *The Divine Comedy*, John Milton's *Paradise Lost*, Marcel Proust's *Remembrance of Things Past*, Thomas Mann's *Magic Mountain*, James Joyce's *Ulysses*, T. S. Eliot's *Wasteland*, and the majority of the oeuvre of John Barth.[2] Following are two swipes at "passing knowledge":

---

2. John Barth is the below-the-radar post-modernist whose name doesn't necessarily roll off the tongue the same way that, say, Thomas Pynchon, or Don Delillo, or, for that matter, Robert Coover does. Hailed as a writer's writer (he writes mostly about writing), he has two large and unyielding books of which one should be aware. They are *Giles Goat-Boy* and *The Sot-Weed Factor*.

LITERATURE

## Really Large Unyielding Work #1: Dante Alighieri (1265–1321) and *The Divine Comedy* (1307–1321)

First, know that the works as a whole are *The Divine Comedy* or *La Divina Commedia*. "The Inferno" is just one part; there's also "Purgatorio" and "Paradiso." People tend to walk around with a vague concept of Dante's version of hell, the nine circles and all that jazz, but rare is the person who knows the distinctions among the circles and in which circle each sinner theoretically belongs. Here are some obvious choices to help you get the hierarchy right so that the next time you want to suggest where your lawyer/accountant/stockbroker should be spending eternity, you'll be sure to have it right.

| CIRCLE | SIN | RESIDENTS |
|---|---|---|
| First Circle Limbo | Decent but Non-Christian Souls | The Blue Meanies |
| Second Circle | Lustful | Wilt Chamberlain[3] Gene Simmons (KISS)[4] 47% of the World Wide Web[5] |

3. In Chamberlain's autobiography he suggested that he had slept with 20,000 women. Doing the math, that works out to roughly three a day for twenty years.
4. Gene Simmons of KISS—the rock equivalent of Mr. Chamberlain.
5. The approximate percentage who view laptops as a PDS—Pornography Delivery Service.

| Third Circle | Gluttonous | Homer Simpson |
| | | Hagar the Horrible |
| Fourth Circle | The Avaricious and the Prodigal | Orson Welles |
| | | John D. Rockefeller |
| Fifth Circle | The Wrathful | J. Edgar Hoover |
| | | Richard Nixon |
| | | The Republican National Party[6] |
| | | Television Preachers |
| | | Professional Wrestlers |
| Sixth Circle | The Heretics | Jim Morrison |
| | | Kenny from *South Park* |
| | | Michael Jackson[7] |
| Seventh Circle | The Violent | The NHL |
| | | The NFL |
| | | Moammar Gadhafi |
| | | Idi Amin |
| | | Slobodan Milosevic |
| | | Radavan Karadic |
| | | The Heroes of Mortal Kombat |

---

6. Lee Atwater may be dead, but nothing can ever right the wrongs done to Michael Dukakis in the name of getting George Bush in office.
7. While it would be possible to place Michael Jackson in any of the many circles of hell, he is in the sixth (and lowest possible for nonviolent offenders) for selling pieces of the Beatles catalog to Nike for use in TV commercials.

| Eighth Circle | The Fraudulent | Martin R. Frankel[8] Plastic Surgeons Cosmetic Plastic Surgery Patients |
| --- | --- | --- |
| Ninth Circle | The Treacherous | Benedict Arnold |

## Really Large Unyielding Work #2: Marcel Proust and *À la Recherche du Temps Perdu* (*Remembrance of Things Past*)

You could actually read Proust, and who doesn't want to sit down with a three-volume set chronicling life at the dawn of the twentieth century in rural France, a three-volume set that deals with the fluid nature of time, the irrationality of love, and the psychological motivations of humans? Or you could pick up Alain De Botton's *How Proust Can Change Your Life: Not a Novel*, an extended meditation on exactly that. Or you could read the following paragraph and come to understand what is meant by a "Proustian" experience.

Early on in the first volume, in a section called "Swann's Way," Proust, upon smelling a madeleine,[9] drifts back to his childhood. This scent, this wafting aroma of madeleine, so vividly connects Proust to his childhood, so incredibly forces upon him recollections

8. Frankel is the fellow who bilked the pope and the insurance companies out of several hundreds of millions of dollars, only to be hunted down and captured in a German hotel some three months later.
9. A madeleine is essentially a Twinkie without the cream filling. (This might cause you to say "My God, what is a Twinkie without the cream filling?" And then you remember: Oh yes, the French.)

of such intensity that when one smells something and it triggers a specific memory, it is generally referred to as a Proustian experience.[10]

---

» *Things That Might Be*
*Referred to as Proustian*

The smell of freshly cut grass

A certain perfume (Oddly enough in a non-scientific study of college-educated men between the ages of twenty-five and forty, it was discovered that the perfume most likely to trigger a Proustian memory was Coco by Chanel.)

Patchouli oil

---

» *Things That Definitely May*
*Be Associative but Are Not Proustian*

The smell of gasoline
The smell of burned flesh
That smell of dried beer in the floorboards
A golden retriever's damp fur

---

## Reference the Minor Works of the Major Authors

Working under the pretense that if you know the minor work you *must* be familiar with the major one, it never hurts to get friendly with smaller works of larger authors.

---

10. There is the corollary notion for music. It is commonly referred to as a "Freebirdian" experience, "Freebird" being a Lynyrd Skynyrd song from the early seventies that triggers memories of junior high and high school dances. It can refer to any piece of music, popular and otherwise, and the transportive power of this medium.

Take Herman Melville and the short story "Bartleby the Scrivener." You may (or may not) have read *Moby Dick,* in which case you've either forgotten everything or you never learned it in the first place. In either scenario, feigning Melville scholarship might be more easily accomplished by referring to "Bartleby the Scrivener." The full title of which is "Bartleby the Scrivener: A Story of Wall Street."

Bartleby is a scrivener in a Wall Street house. The primary enterprise of said house is the pursuit of the almighty Coin. One day, Bartleby's employer inquires, "Will you tell me, Bartleby, where you were born?" To which Bartleby replies, "I would prefer not to."

The employer then asks, "Will you tell me *any thing* about yourself?" To which Bartleby again replies, "I would prefer not to."

This goes on for some time, and to each new request, whether it be to engage in his chosen profession of copying documents (for that is what a scrivener does), or to simply vacate the premises, Bartleby responds in similar fashion, "I would prefer not to."

His defiant and relentlessly polite stance serves as both literary reference-dropping and a perfectly legitimate way to respond to any and all questions. Think of the possibilities:

Would you go get me another drink?

I would prefer not to.

Tell me about your job.

I would prefer not to.

Were you to marry the cadence of the words with the appropriate dose of millennial irony you would find yourself aligned perfectly with Bartleby, the great apathetic anti-hero of the nineteenth century.

## Accurately Quoting Shakespeare Is Rarely (if Ever) a Bad Thing

As such, here are a few gems from the works, and situations where they seem most apt. For credibility's sake, remember the play, scene, and act numbers—at the very least recall the play. (Impact is at least two times as great if you can recall play-scene-act.)

» On Getting across the Room to Get a Drink

"Once more into the breach, dear friends, once more."
—*Henry V,* III:1

» On What to Do with the Surplus of Legal Talent at the End of the Century

"The first thing we do let's kill all the lawyers."
—*II Henry VI,* IV:2

---

» *Shakespeare on Lawyers*

*Should you either be a lawyer or be simply fond of said profession, recall that the preceding line was written with an eye toward abolishing all civil liberties. Wipe out the lawyers and there will be no one to argue for the people.*

---

» On Evil Heading in Your Direction

"By the pricking of my thumbs,
  Something wicked this way comes." —*Macbeth*, IV:1

» On Wishing to End It with Your S. O. Once and for All

If thou dost marry, I'll give thee this plague for thy
dowry: be thou as chaste as ice, as pure as snow, thou
shalt not escape calumny. Get thee to a nunnery, go:
farewell. Or, if thou wilt needs marry, marry a fool; for
wise men know well enough what monsters you make
of them. To a nunnery, go, and quickly too. Farewell.
                                           —*Hamlet*, III:1

Or of course you could stick with the short version,
which is: "Get Thee to a Nunnery!"      —*Hamlet*, III:1

» On Advising a Friend What to Do after a Breakup
  (Or Any Great Moral Crisis)

"This above all: to thine own self be true. . . ."
                                           —*Hamlet*, I:3

» On Spilling Red Wine on White Linen

"Out, damned spot! out, I say."

                                           —*Macbeth*, V:1

» A Remarkably Cute Way to Refer to, Um, Scrumping

"I am one, sir, that comes to tell you your daughter
  and the Moor are now making the beast with two backs."
                                           —*Othello*, I:1

» On the Plight of Humans

(This should be said while looking up and off into the distance, preferably presenting a three-quarters profile to whomever you may be addressing and with a glass in hand—the grand gesture is highly recommended.)

All the world's a stage,
And all the men and women merely players.
They have their exits and their entrances,
And one man in his time plays many parts,
His acts being seven ages.

—*As You Like It,* II:7

» On Jousting, Verbally or Otherwise, with an Adversary

"Lay on, Macduff,
And damn'd be him that first cries, 'Hold, enough!'"

—*Macbeth,* V:8

# Understand the Wonder and Joy That Is Jonathan Swift, Master Satirist (1667–1745)

Swift, best known as the author of *Gulliver's Travels,* was possessed of a deft and sure-footed gift for satire. And while it is *Gulliver* for which he may be best remembered, a pamphlet he wrote called *A Modest Proposal* shows how deliciously perverse he could be. In this slim work he suggested that the Irish, withering under the economic hardship of the times, should sell their children for the wealthy to then eat—thereby being relieved of the burden of rearing them *and,* at the same time, turning a general profit.

When you wish to suggest an original and potentially controversial plan of action, one that might be ironic in nature, you can't go wrong in suggesting, "I have a Modest Proposal. . ."

## Freely Employ Mildly Esoteric French References at the Dinner Table

The French, with their devotion to delights epicurean and *joie de vivre,* are, in essence, the ideal reference point for the chat-set, the cocktail environment, the salon.

Look at Émile Zola. If you haven't read Zola, just picture Tom Wolfe, author of *The Bonfire of the Vanities* and *A Man in Full,* take away the sartorial splendor, throw a few pounds on him, slap him in a time machine, and send him back to nineteenth-century France. (For those keeping score, Zola first made it big with the "life in the mines really sucks" novel *Germinal.*) But for our purposes, it is Zola-the-letter-writer as opposed to Zola-the-author with whom we are most concerned.

When you know who has done one of the following: eaten the last crabcake, downed the last beer, had the last sip of fabulous wine, or spilled on the carpet, point a finger in their direction and say, *"J'accuse."* Which, of course, means "I accuse you" in French. It harks back to a scathing letter that Zola wrote berating the French government for keeping an innocent, Captain Alfred Dreyfus, behind bars on trumped-up charges of treason. It's best if you can execute this as a grand gesture: Place the right index finger just above your heart and then *snap!* your arm straight, proclaiming, *"J'accuse!"*

## Utilize Adjectival Forms of Favorite Authors You Haven't Read in Some Time

*Machiavellian*—Niccolò Machiavelli's *The Prince* remains a resource guide to help anyone make it to the top of the ladder—corporate, social, or playground. If you're throwing the adjectival form around, it's usually best applied as a backhanded compliment. For example:

> On Hearing of Your Friends' Vicious and Triumphant Powerplay at His/Her Place of Employ "How deliciously Machiavellian of you."

*Utopian*—When discussing ideas, concepts, or sentiments that are not wholly clothed in the reality of today's world, the Utopian sentiment always works. It is the literary equivalent of the old throw-away "looking at the world through rose-colored glasses."

> On Dismissing the Optimism of a Friend "Oh Timmy, he has a rather Utopian way of looking at things."

*Rabelaisian*—As in François Rabelais, the French author of *Gargantua* and *Pantagruel*.

Picture a Gallic Orson Welles and late-model Gerard Depardieu as a father-and-son team gorging themselves on wine, women, and song in the French countryside and you get the idea what the books are about. As the work is devoted primarily and abundantly to pursuits of the flesh, *Rabelaisian* is an extremely appropriate term, usually referring to one's appetites, be they sexual, gastronomic, or alcoholic.

On a Friend's Propensity to Booze It Up
"Let us say he has a—how shall I put this—
Rabelaisian appetite for the bottle."

*Quixotic*—Of or pertaining to the skewed worldview of Miguel Cervantes' mad knight—tilting at windmills and all that. Quixotic is one of the better ways to refer to any quest—romantic or otherwise—that is doomed to defeat.

On Being Told by Friends That You Will Not Get the Girl of Your Dreams
"I would prefer to think of it not as an abject failure, but rather as having been a quixotic enterprise."

---

## » Quixotic: The 174-Point Scrabble Play

*The best possible play in the Milton Bradley board game Scrabble would be to form the word* QUIXOTIC, *with the Q and the X going across Triple Letter Scores, while the whole of the word covers a Double Word Score and you get the Bingo! bonus of 50 for using all your tiles.*

*The sum total of this is a whopping 174 points. The beauty is that it is a quixotic act in and of itself, as it is hopelessly romantic and idealistic to believe, even if one were to play Scrabble every day for the rest of one's life, that one would draw the tiles and find the board positioned in such a way as to allow for spelling it out.*

*Q=10   U=1   I=1   X=8   O=1   T=1   I=1   C=3*

---

*Joycean*—Pertaining to that meandering quality that Joyce can sometimes seem to have when you're not quite following the whole "stream-of-consciousness" spiel. A polite way of suggesting that somebody is rambling on in an obtuse fashion. Cousin to both "meandering" and "discursive."

> On Trying to Comprehend Some Random Stream-of-Consciousness Spiel
> "I admit there is a certain Joycean logic to what you're saying."

*Kafkaesque*—The author's trademark style so specifically captures a certain kind of twentieth-century nightmarish dysfunction that his name has come to be synonymous with the labyrinthine and inefficient workings of bureaucracy. Nearly all dealings with any branch of government or institution—the IRS, the DMV, your HMO, your credit-card company—are, in some facet or another, Kafkaesque. In recounting a visit to any one of the above institutions, feel free to invoke the term. It is, in essence, a nightmare high-brow version of "Catch-22." E.g., were you to receive a random e-mail addressed to you—but it wasn't really you—and then have the East German Secret Police burst in, steal your computer, and accuse you of stealing state secrets, that would be Kafkaesque.

## When the Going Gets Competitive, the Competitive Turn to Virginia Woolf—Alternatively, Know One Passage in One Book as Well as You Know Your Name

Invariably, when one person gets together with another person, competition and one-upmanship rear their ugly heads. At this point you can find aid in the work of

Virginia Woolf. In a passage from *To the Lighthouse*, a character, one Mr. Ramsay, seeks to define himself. In his mind Mr. Ramsay believes that the greatest of great men, "one in a generation, one in a thousand million," is able to reach the letter Z.[11] Arriving at that letter, arriving at that letter is like climbing Everest without benefit of oxygen, scoring the winning touchdown in the Super Bowl, winning the Nobel prize for pioneering cancer research. It is the ultimate act that very few can attain.

Mr. Ramsay, try as he may, is only able to get to the letter Q. Though he pushes and prods and strives, though he yearns, burns, desires, covets, and wishes for greater, he can get no farther than Q. He very nearly touches R—he knows it's there—he's close, but . . . it's out of reach. This is a small, out-of-the-way bit in a celebrated though out-of-the-way book. It's simple to remember, and invoking it suggests a level of self-awareness as to your place in the world, the mark of all highly evolved beings.

*Humble Version*: "Do you know that bit in *To the Lighthouse*, that bit where the guy, what's his name, Mr. Ramsay, is trying desperately to get to R, trying to get to R, as if getting to R would make him more of a man, as if getting to R would and could be the grand goal of his entire existence? I don't know, man, sometimes, sometimes, I would just settle for P."

---

11. Z being a metaphor for the rarified status that only the greatest of the great achieve, an ineffable *je ne sais quoi* that few if any have ever arrived at. (For example, the author believes that Michael Jordan, late of the Chicago Bulls, may possibly have reached Z, but Tom Cruise hasn't.)

*Less Humble*: "You know that bit in *To the Lighthouse*, that bit where the guy is trying desperately to get to R, like R makes him some kind of something special? I mean, what a slacker. Talk about lacking ambition. He couldn't even get to R! That's just the eighteenth letter, that's seventy-five percent of the way there. At the very least, at the very least, shouldn't he have shot for V?"

## Be Able to Make Wide Sweeping Generalizations about Things Like "Hell in Literature" or the "Tradition of Americans and the Road Novel"

Show off your encyclopedic knowledge and critical faculties by being able to draw parallels throughout literature.

### Wide Sweeping Generalization #1:

Many a literary great has taken a stab at the miseries, wonders, and wilds of the underworld, or at least since the moment all things went to seed when Eve bit the apple. Below are four guys who knew their way around Hell, the Devil, and trafficking in the fates of the mortal soul.

| AUTHOR | TITLE | DEVIL'S NAME | HOW HELL IS SHOWCASED | MODERN RELEVANCE |
|--------|-------|--------------|-----------------------|------------------|
| Dante Alighieri 13th Century | *La Divina Commedia* (*The Divine Comedy*) | Unspoken | Dante journeys up through Hell (the *Inferno*), Purgatory (*Purgatorio*) and on into Paradise (*Paradiso*). | Gives a geospatia map of damnation, which can be handy when you're planning the afterlife. |

# LITERATURE

| AUTHOR | TITLE | DEVIL'S NAME | HOW HELL IS SHOWCASED | MODERN RELEVANCE |
|--------|-------|--------------|-----------------------|------------------|
| John Milton 17th Century | *Paradise Lost*[12] | Beelzebub | The Devil, having been kicked out of heaven, has a field day down in Hell. | "Better to reign in Hell than serve in Heav'n." |
| Johann Wolfgang von Goethe[13] | *Faust* | Mephisto-pheles | A doctor makes the proverbial deal with the Devil in exchange for knowledge and experience. | The Faustian Bargain is the best metaphor going for fame, celebrity, and riches. You trade your soul, you get fame, celebrity, and riches. This is the paparazzi's argument for taking pictures of people landing at airports, with their children as they emerge from the hospital, and from helicopters at private weddings and on nude beaches in the Caribbean.[14] Feel free to use this notion whenever you |

12. There is a brilliant moment in the film *Animal House* that sums up Milton rather nicely. In it the professor played by Donald Sutherland, while addressing the disinterested student body, says, "Mrs. Milton found him boring too. He's a little bit long-winded, doesn't translate very well into our generation. And his jokes are terrible."
13. Pronounced GER-tuh—like the way Sade is pronounced SHAR-day.
14. Dividing people into two camps can be a dangerous and petty thing. But it can safely be said that there are two kinds of people: those who understand "the Faustian Bargain" and those who don't. Those who do understand realize that unmerited success can often translate into abject disaster.

| AUTHOR | TITLE | DEVIL'S NAME | HOW HELL IS SHOWCASED | MODERN RELEVANCE |
|--------|-------|--------------|----------------------|------------------|
| | | | | want—it is great linguistic currency. |
| Matt Groening | *Life in Hell* | Akbar and /or Jeff | Two very funny-looking guys who wear fezzes and who may or may not be gay spend an eternity making each other miserable. | Precursor to *The Simpsons*. Sometimes forgotten as the place where Groening got his start and a great study on the dynamic of two people who hate each other because they love each other. |

## Wide Sweeping Generalization #2:

The notion of Wide Open Spaces resides at the center of the American Literary Tradition. Three guys who helped define this most American of ethos had their own special take, their own patois, their own way of writing not just the Great American Novel, but the Great American Road Novel.

| | NOVEL | PROTAGONISTS | MEANS OF TRANSPORTATION | WHAT IT SAYS ABOUT AMERICA | CONTROVERSY |
|--|-------|--------------|------------------------|---------------------------|-------------|
| Mark Twain | *Huckleberry Finn* | Huckleberry Finn and the runaway slave Jim | A raft floating on the Mississippi | An attack on "adult culture" and the various shortcomings of "growing up" | Racist! Or not? |

| | NOVEL | PROTAGONISTS | MEANS OF TRANSPOR- TATION | WHAT IT SAYS ABOUT AMERICA | CONTROVERSY |
|---|---|---|---|---|---|
| Jack Kerouac | *On the Road* | Sal Paradise (Jack Kerouac) and Dean Moriarty (Neal Cassady) | Buses, hitching, Cadillacs, trains, and hoofing it | It's a big place, and dreamers and deadbeats can make the most of it. | Misogynist! Or not? |
| Hunter S. Thompson | *Fear and Loathing in Las Vegas* | Hunter S. Thompson and his attorney, whose name is rarely mentioned but happens to be Oscar | The Great Red Shark —a 1972 Cadillac | Hallucinogens plus Las Vegas plus gonzo spirit equals a sterling literary career, or the American Dream is dead. | Great Literature! Or not? |

## Never Underestimate the Power of a Good Literary Anecdote

What to do when everybody is already so intimate with an author that anything that you can say, unless you are a Ph.D., would only be reciting the obvious? Tell tales of their lives—it just might prove to be more interesting.

### Ernest Hemingway and His Editor[15]

Hem, as he was known to some, was fond of using words that, while in the vernacular, had not yet made it

---

15. Hemingway and Fitzgerald shared an editor. And no, they did not share anything else.

into the rarified pages of literature. Consequently, his editor at Scribner's, one Maxwell Perkins, was continually having to discuss potential changes to the author's work. Perkins, knowing that he needed to go over some, um, ribald language with Hemingway, jotted down the potentially offensive words *shit, fuck,* and *piss* on the nearest bit of scrap nearby—his datebook.

As the story goes, Perkins's notoriously uptight and conservative boss happened to wander into Perkins's office and spy these words scribbled in the margin of his agenda. Upon seeing this, he turned to his editor and said, "Max, if you need to remind yourself to do these things, maybe it's time you took a vacation."

## Gustave Flaubert on His Sexuality

Flaubert wrote so brilliantly about women, about their desires, their thoughts, and their perceptions, that his own sexuality was often called into question.

On one such occasion the following exchange took place:

"*Monsieur Flaubert, êtes-vous un homosexuel?*"

(Monsieur Flaubert, are you a homosexual?)

"*Mais non, je suis un lesbien.*"

(But of course not. I am a lesbian.)

## Know the Life Story of at Least One Fairly Random International Author or, Rejoice in Getting a Chance to Say the Word *Seppuku* (Sape-puu-kuu)

Sick of the traditional writer's life story and the pitfalls of that profession? Here's a twist on commingling art and life that doesn't deal with alcohol, personal short-comings, or any frailty of the spirit.

Yukio Mishima (1925–1970), the Japanese author of the *Sea of Fertility* tetralogy (*Spring Snow, Runaway Horses, The Temple of Dawn,* and *The Decay of the Angel*), expired in grandiose, dramatic fashion.

*Why Anybody May Have Heard of Him*:
For the literary record, Mishima was an author who bridged the gap from traditional Japanese writing to a more modern, Western style, synthesizing traditional Japanese culture into a post-war aesthetic.

But it is Mishima's life and career as a national figure and philosopher that make him even more interesting. During his lifetime he formed an ultra-nationalist cadre. Their goal: to restore the Japanese emperor to his rightful throne.

*Why You Would Want to Talk about Him*:
Upon finishing *The Decay of the Angel,* the fourth book in his tetralogy *Sea of Fertility,* Mishima, along with his cadre, paid a visit to a local army base. As a well-respected and famous person, he was promptly granted access to the very highest officer, whom he promptly took hostage. Mishima went forth and exhorted the troops to join him in a battle to restore the emperor. He was laughed off the stage, returned to the base head-quarters, and, along with his cadre, committed ritual suicide, or *seppuku.*

It's an over-the-top example of what happens when a person takes his beliefs *all the way*. It illustrates how intertwined Mishima's life's work—tales about the decay of traditional Japan into a vast, meaningless, cultureless, sterile void—became with his life, which was an ongoing battle to combat that selfsame decay. So take it light and have fun with *seppuku* or go heavy and talk about having the kind of conviction to carry even the most extreme actions to their bitter end.

## And Remember: It Could Always Be Worse

Perhaps no line in literature can put in better perspective a bad day than the following:

"As Gregor Samsa awoke one morning from uneasy dreams he found himself transformed in his bed into a gigantic insect."

# LINGUISTIC INTERLUDE III: FRENCH

*A French phrase has, over time, proven to be one of the more sure-fire ways to improve the degree to which your punditry may be appreciated. For your consumption, terms and concepts of the Gallic way.*

»*Le quart d'heure de politesse* (Le kar duhr de poe-lee-tess)
Actual tardiness doesn't truly begin until you are more than fifteen minutes late. *Le quart d'heure de politesse*, translated literally, means "the quarter hour of politeness," a sort of grace period within which you are allowed to arrive. If you are late but within a fifteen-minute time frame, you are, as the saying goes, casually late.

»*L'esprit d'escalier* (Leh-spree des-kah-lee-ay)
Literally translated, this means "stairway of the wit or mind." If you are insulted or subject to a particularly searing piece of wit and you think of the comeback some twenty minutes later when it will do you no good, you then are experiencing *l'esprit d'escalier.*

»*Être bien dans son peau* (Et-ruh bee-en dohn sohn poh)
A French way of saying "I'm rocking" or "I feel good." To be in one's skin. The first person would be *Je suis bien dans ma peau*. The third person, for a girlfriend who has come into her own, *Elle est bien dans sa peau*. Or, for a guyfriend, *Il est bien dans sa peau.*

»Plus ça change, plus c'est la même chose
(Ploo sa shahn-je, ploo say lah mem shows)
French for "The more things change the more they stay the same." It's not necessary to add *plus c'est la même chose*; you can simply say with a resigned air, "*Plus ça change . . .*"

»*L'un de ces jours* . . . (Lahn duh say jeurs)
Literally translated, "One of these days." It is the hipster French way to say, "I'll catch you on the flip side."

»*Au secours* (Oh suh-kors)
"Help!" as in when thrown into a dark, churning sea. Useful when standing next to company you don't wish to keep, or when being dragged away forcefully, either by having your ear boxed or your shirt-sleeve pulled: "*Au secours! Au secours!*"

»*Chaud devant* (Show duh-vahn)
"Hot behind you!" What is mouthed as waiters and cocktail servers try to navigate crowded French restaurants. An obnoxious French version of "Coming through!"

# CELLULOID HEROEſ

"Nobody knows anything. . . ."
—William Goldman[1]
(Author, Screenwriter, and
Hollywood Legend)

"Los Angeles is where the dysfunc-
tional come to misunderstand
each other."    —Anonymous

---

1. William Goldman possesses a perspective on Lotusland that is both unique and informed, as he has been a leading screenwriter for over thirty years. His credits include but are not limited to *The Marathon Man, Butch Cassidy and the Sundance Kid, All the President's Men,* and *The Princess Bride.*

> ## » A Historically Based Hypothesis as to Why Hollywood Is Just Like High School

*The founders of the major studios all emigrated from small Eastern European shtetls[2] within 100 miles of each other. As the 1800s came to a close, William Fox (20th Century Fox) and Adolph Zukor (Paramount) came over from Hungary. Jack, Harry, Albert, and Sam Warner (the Warners in Warner Bros.), as well as Samuel B. Goldfish (became the Goldwyn in Metro-Goldwyn-Mayer), emigrated from Poland. And the Mayer (Louis B., to be exact) came from Minsk.*

*Their spirited rivalry in the early years of the film industry infused the town with a nervous, manic energy and the trademark mind-set of paranoia, back-biting, and hubris. This is but the oldest of the many theories as to why Hollywood is very much like high school, just with bigger egos and more money.*

## It's a Company Town—Three Indispensable Bits of Left Coast Culture

### 1. Everybody Has a Screenplay They're Working On....

If you're within a 150-mile radius of Hollywood and Vine, the third question out of someone's mouth usually is, "What's your screenplay about?" If you asked the question first it would be too forward, second would make it look like you were just waiting so it wouldn't be the first, but third is just fine. *Everybody* in La-La has an idea for a screenplay; it's as de rigueur as sunglasses and valet parking.

---

2. Shtetl—Yiddish for "burg."

## 2. Hollywood Is Just Like High School, Only with More Money and Bigger Egos

The nervous energy of a fourteen-year-old boy concerned about his looks, body, and status has its adult equivalent in the twenty-seven-year-old talent agent/manager concerned about his looks, body, and status.

The similarities between Hollywood and high school run deep and consist of the tyranny of popularity, the virulence of gossip, and the frenetic emotional intensity of adolescence.

The parallels run equally deep. The Studio Execs are the preppies in loafers, the Movie Stars are the jocks, the Indy Film Folk are the stoners/artists, and the Finance Mavens are the geeks.

## 3. Refer to Stars by Their First Names

All talent in the film biz should be referred to by first names, as in "Jack was out on the links the other day" or "Did you see Warren[3] at the commissary this morning?" Even if one has never met Jack or Warren or, for that matter, Michelle, Jodie, or Meg, it is de rigueur to refer to them in this fashion. Cheese points are awarded for nicknames; "Leo" doesn't count, but "Marty" for Martin Scorsese (Skor-SEH-zee) does. And refer to Lauren Bacall as "Betty" if you dare.

"Suits," the executive team, are hailed by their family name. The most prominent example of this trend is the recently created Dreamworks SKG prominently featuring the names Spielberg, Katzenberg, Geffen. Of course, as

---

3. Warren Beatty and Shirley MacLaine are brother and sister.

always, the exception proves the rule and when Spielberg steps behind the camera he becomes simply "Steven."

### First Movie Camera:

*The cinematographe (hence the term* cinema*), invented by Frenchman Louis Lumière, 1895. Thomas Edison had one too, but Lumière's was more portable.*

### First Narrative Film:

The Great Train Robbery, *1903*[4]

### First Talking Film:

The Jazz Singer, *1927. Script had only 350 words, less than your "What I Did Last Summer" essay in third grade (but there were those six songs plus Al Jolson).*

## Talking Movies

## A Very Short List: No-Brainers to Tuck under Your Belt

The baseline of all movie conversations is seminal films. Here are a few chosen for very specific reasons, complete with ways you can refer to them, and why they are important.

---

4. Whenever a new medium (radio, TV, the Internet) arises, talk inevitably turns to *The Great Train Robbery*. Why? Because when it was first shown people were said to flee the theaters for fear that the train was coming off the screen. It represents the moment a medium arrives.

## The First Feature Film, 1915: D. W. Griffith's
## *The Birth of a Nation*

*Important Reason #1*:
The next time you walk out of another three-hour-plus opus of which forty or so minutes could have been cut, be sure to blame D. W. Griffith. It's been epic-envy ever since Griffith unleashed his 3 1/2-hour *silent* masterpiece that launched the entire movie business nearly overnight. (He also managed to stir up considerable protest: Positive portrayals on screen of the KKK didn't go over well, even in 1915.)

*Important Reason #2*:
Griffith is the original Hollywood heartbreak story. Having virtually created the movie business as we know it today, he died penniless in a fleabag Hollywood hotel room.

# The Ensemble Film, 1975: Robert Altman's *Nashville*

» Why *Nashville*:

Enlisting legions of talented brand-name actors at cost is the trademark of both Robert Altman and Woody Allen.

---

» *The Whole Out-of-Date Thing*

*A great cocktail-party trick is to discuss an out-of-date work, be it an out-of-print book, an out-of-issue CD, or, in this case, the Altman film* California Split, *which somehow, someway, never made it to video. Talk about how much you liked the film, specifically the scene where Segal tries to convince Gould of the emptiness of the big win. Suggest that it was so bleak that even thinking about it creeps you out.*

---

> ## » *The Seventies Hit Parade*
>
> *The seventies are recognized as the heyday of a certain kind of gritty, personal American film. When speaking of the seventies, wistful is the appropriate tone while waxing rhapsodic about:* Badlands, Shampoo, Mean Streets, Chinatown, Five Easy Pieces, American Graffiti.

*The Player* introduced Robert Altman to anyone under forty, but stick with *Nashville* when his name pops up. *Nashville* is the hidden gem in the hit parade of seventies films. Liking it suggests a subtle kind of film erudition, one that appreciates a sprawling improvisational ensemble cast, meandering yet intersecting story lines, and a film where Lily Tomlin is the biggest star.

## » How to Talk about It:

Express amazement at how deftly Altman manages to link twenty-four separate characters, a country-and-western musical, and a documentary on the corrupt electoral process in the U.S.A. (The film came out right after Watergate.) To really stretch it out, comment on the naturalistic style (nobody seems to be doing all that much *acting*) and comment that watching the twenty-five-year-old videotape only adds to the cinema verité quality of authenticity. To contextualize your comments, mention that Paul Thomas Anderson of *Boogie Nights* and *Magnolia* has a certain "Altmanesque" style.

## Sci-Fi Dystopia and That Whole Director's Cut Thing, 1983: Ridley Scott's *Blade Runner*

## » Why *Blade Runner*:

Like van Gogh's *Sunflowers* or Stravinsky's *Rite of Spring,* neither of which was well received when it first appeared, *Blade Runner* came out of the gates limping. But today it is hailed as a sci-fi masterpiece, the benchmark of a dystopian future for works ranging from cyberpunk novels to apocalyptic video games.

What happened? Time and a re-release in 1991 triggered the long, slow march to credibility, while at the same time it unleashed the whole "Director's Cut" thing upon the mainstream.

---

### » *Harrison Ford: The Twentieth-Century Box Office God*

*Before Harrison Ford became the biggest box-office star of all time—with over $2 billion to his credit—he was a carpenter. Though he only did this for a brief period of time, there are thousands of people who proudly say, "Oh yeah, Harrison Ford built me these cabinets."*

---

### » How to Talk about It:

Know that the big difference between the original and the Director's Cut is the voice-over, or v.o. In the original, Ridley Scott was kicked off the film and Harrison Ford was forced into doing a hackneyed voice-over.[5] The later director's cut omits the v.o., and, in this case, is generally considered to be a better film.

---

5. The v.o. is in fact a much-reviled expository technique that in most cases suggests the director or studio head replacing the director had no clue what to do with the picture and resorted to the v.o.

As for the film, remark on the similarities between Ford's lone gunman Deckard and Gary Cooper's lone gunman in *High Noon*, and the notion that Scott managed to make a film noir—all grit, shadows, and bleakness—set in the future, which previously had been viewed as shiny, sterile, and wonderful.

» High-Brow Cheese Points:

*Blade Runner* is based on the Philip K. Dick[6] novel *Do Androids Dream of Electric Sheep?*

## The Madness That Is Moviemaking, 1991: *Apocalypse Now* and *Hearts of Darkness*: *A Filmmaker's Apocalypse*

» Why *Hearts*:

More than just "Look, here's Francis in his underwear,"[7] *Hearts of Darkness*, a documentary film shot by Coppola's wife, Eleanor, during the filming of *Apocalypse Now*, is a descent into the darker, less glamorous regions of creativity, artistic passion, and costs-be-damned filmmaking.

*Apocalypse Now* began as a simple Vietnam War film loosely based on Joseph Conrad's *Heart of Darkness*. A winner in the "truth is stranger than fiction" sweepstakes, the film *Hearts of Darkness* opens with the notion that legions of directors, including Orson Welles, had tried to adapt the short story to film but never licked it;

---

6. Philip K. Dick, now dead, is the leading intellectual sci-fi writer. Another film based on his work includes *Total Recall*.
7. There are shots throughout the documentary of Francis Ford Coppola at the typewriter in his underwear.

they just couldn't figure out how to make the translation from page to screen. *Hearts* then goes on to follow Coppola as he tries desperately to stave off creditors, the Philippine army, and self-doubt, all to get to his own personal "Heart of Darkness": the truth.

---

### » *Movies and War—*
### *Twin Sons of Different Mothers*

*Filmmaking and warfare can be viewed as remarkably similar activities. They both cost tons of money. Large groups of people assemble under difficult, stressful, and life-threatening situations to achieve a common goal. In the case of war, people are seeking to achieve peace. In the case of making movies, they're trying to get a piece.*

---

### » How to Talk about It:

Some of the highlights that are captured in *Hearts*:

- Martin Sheen has a heart attack and Coppola is livid that the news gets leaked back to the States: "I don't care if Marty dies; you don't go tell the press about it."
- A monsoon strikes—and Coppola, thinking it's just heavy rain, wants to shoot in it.
- Helicopters on loan from the Philippine armed forces continually get called away to fight insurrectionist rebels in the hills.
- Dennis Hopper is at the peak of his self-confessed drug-induced mania.

- Marlon Brando, the lead and linchpin of the final scene, has not only not read *Heart of Darkness* (as he had promised he would) but he has not even looked at the script!

Suggest you had a hard time deciding which was the more twisted situation, Coppola talking to an incoherent Hopper who can't speak because he's jacked up on drugs, or Brando, who can't communicate because... well... because...

## Film Geek Cheese Points:

For remembering that Laurence Fishburne was fourteen years old when he made *Apocalypse Now*. At that point he was still known as Larry.

---

### » *More Film Geek Cheese Points*

*For the obscure and knowing out there, throw in the group Tangerine Dream, whose score for the James Caan film* Thief *is considered a sparkling gem of the field. If you can't remember the film* Thief *or have never heard the score, know then that Tangerine Dream scored* Risky Business. *Just think of the train scene in which Rebecca De Mornay and Tom Cruise ride the El until dawn while Tangerine Dream plays in the background.*

## General Movie Terms

»Cinematography—Literally, how the picture looks.
Cinematography is a blend of lighting, camera angles, and what can loosely be termed "visual style." Cinematographers tend to have strange complicated foreign names such as Sven Nykvist, Vittorio Storaro, and Vilmos Zsigmond, a notion that was riffed on in the Kevin Bacon film *The Big Picture*.[8]
Rule of Thumb: If a movie is gorgeous, thank the cinematographer. When discussing cinematography, feel free to use words like *stunning, brilliant, masterful.*

»Score—Not to be confused with the Sound Track.
The Sound Track is a collection of songs that appear in a film, while the Score is everything that goes on during the film. The Score is that wonderfully moody thing that moves the film along, heightening moments of tension where appropriate, and softening you up for the scare of your life in horror films. Think of the score in the same way you think of dialogue in a script: The better it is, the less you even know it's there.

»Set Design/Production Design—Think of the *Batman* movies with their dark, otherworldly feel, or, alternatively, a Merchant-Ivory film. Production designers are well compensated interior decorators using slightly more perishable materials—the sets disappear when the movie does. Save your comments on the Production or Set Design for period pictures, and yes, *Boogie Nights* counts as a period piece.

---

8. *The Big Picture* predates Kevin Bacon's resurgence as a cultural icon of mass import due to the Six Degrees of Kevin Bacon game. It also has a searing hysterical and uncredited performance by Martin Short as a talent agent. His best line: "I've read almost all of your scripts almost all of the way through."

»Rushes—Synonymous with dailies.
The reel from a day's shooting that is then viewed to see how filming has been going. Directors and/or actors have been fired after screenings of the rushes—they can be influential in the overall filmmaking process.

## Polarize a Room with Just Two Words: Oliver and Stone

Oliver Stone might not necessarily be the most controversial director working today; that honorific could go to Harmony Korine, the writer of *Kids* and director of *Gummo*. But on a scale composed of infamy, notoriety, and controversy, Stone ranks at or near the top. A laundry list of potential crimes against film and the American public record that can be attributed to Oliver Stone and his filmmaking techniques:

- Seamlessly mixing documentary with filmed footage and presenting it as if it were one and the same. As a naysayer of Mr. Stone's work you might call him irresponsible. As a fan, you could call his work bravura filmmaking.
- Distorting actual persons and incidents to fit his own agenda. He did this with Jim Garrison, the attorney in *JFK*, and with his iconic Jim Morrison in *The Doors*. Feeling benevolent? Suggest that these are after all movies and Stone is merely a storyteller making the most of his medium. Feeling less generous? Make the point that Stone subverts facts and perverts the truth under the auspices of telling the truth.
- *Natural Born Killers*—is it a video how-to for the Jerry Springer Nation or, as Stone would have us all believe, *satire*?

> ## » Oliver Stone on Oliver Stone
>
> *Oliver Stone has a pretty good sense of humor—especially about himself. Once asked in an interview if he didn't feel guilty about having made most of his money in films about the counterculture, Stone replied, "Guilt, that's a Western thing."*

### Moments in Film That Can Inform Your Reality

»The Garp Theory of Life (the Positive Side of Disaster) from *The World According to Garp*

A biplane crashes into a house at the very moment Garp (Robin Williams) and his wife are looking into buying said house. On the spot he says, "Great, I'll take it." To which the Realtor responds, "But . . ." And Garp says, "What are the odds of anything this terrible ever happening here again?"

»A Nurse Ratched Moment from *One Flew Over the Cuckoo's Nest*: Nurse Ratched (Louise Fletcher) is the malevolent ogre who runs the insane asylum into which Randall McMurphy (Jack Nicholson) is thrown. She controls the environment so tightly, is so patently evil and mean-spirited, that she is the very definition of unyielding authority.

Whenever you find yourself experiencing the most extreme rage and frustration in equal proportion—visual: the angriest dog in the world tugging on an extremely short leash—and it is due to a certain figure lording over you, this can be characterized as a Nurse Ratched moment. E.g. the loan officer watching the clock tick the moments away to five o'clock, when a new, higher prime lending rate will take effect.

»Bringing in the Expert from *Annie Hall*: In *Annie Hall* Woody Allen as Alvy Singer is standing in line at a movie theater and overhearing a total idiot bastardize Marshall McLuhan's theories on the future. Allen is outraged that the guy is butchering McLuhan, at which point Allen turns to the camera and says, "What do you do when you get stuck in a movie line with a guy like this behind you?" Because it's his movie, here's what he does: He pulls McLuhan out of nowhere to dismiss and debunk the idiot. This fantasy sequence is something to hold on to and wish for whenever you are listening to anybody prattle on about something they know nothing about.

## A Few Words on Difference
The Actor and the Movie Star

As with the words *movie* and *film*, so too is there a distinction between Actor and Movie Star. Here's a quick-study guide using De Niro and Pacino as examples.

| | ROBERT "BOB" DE NIRO | AL PACINO | THE WINNER |
|---|---|---|---|
| Despicable Characters Played Well | Jake La Motta in *Raging Bull* —a fat, misongynist pig who is mean to people | Violence has a new name—a guy who yells at the top of his lungs, "My name is Tony Montana," aka "Scarface" | De Niro for the acting; Pacino for the final scene, where he gets shot like 274 times and still won't fall. |
| Cop on the Take Who Didn't Fit In | *Midnight Run*— Chicago cop Jack Walsh, who wouldn't take a bribe so he got run out of Chicago on a rail | Justice has a new name—a guy who yells at the top of his lungs that he's just a cop trying to change the system —"Serpico" | Pacino |

# CELLULOID HEROES

| | ROBERT "BOB" DE NIRO | AL PACINO | THE WINNER |
|---|---|---|---|
| As a Corleone in the *Godfather* Films | As a young Vito, the original Godfather, De Niro is pretty tough. | There's a new Godfather and he yells a lot and is comfortable showing his passionate side | Pacino |
| As an Incarnation of the Devil | De Niro as Louis Cyphre in *Angel Heart* | The Devil incarnate that yells a lot and his name is John Milton—*The Devil's Advocate* | Pacino |
| Best Actor Oscar–Winning Performance | He gains half his body weight and literally becomes a dissolute boxer down on his luck —*Raging Bull*. | A blind guy yells a lot and drives a Ferrari—a passionate vehicle. —*Scent of a Woman* | Two Words: "Hoo-Ha" De Niro |
| Number of Times "Fuck" Is Used in Gangster Film | 246: *Good Fellas* | 206: *Scarface* | The numbers say De Niro |
| Face-to-Face in *Heat* | De Niro plays the softspoken bad guy with the heart of gold—he's got one last score. | Pacino plays the cop who yells a lot with the messed-up personal life—has a better tan in this one. | It's a toss-up: you like De Niro he's your winner; you like Pacino —he's your guy. |

# A Couple Basic Things You Should Know if You're Going to Talk the Talk

## Know That There Are Two Points to the Common Argument as to Why Hollywood Can't Make a Decent Movie

### » 1. Hollywood Is Creatively Bankrupt

Movies cost money, lots of money. Films based on video games, comic books, and TV shows, not to mention sequels and remakes, have, in theory, built-in audiences dying to see "the big-screen adaptation." This quickly turns the Hollywood landscape into one that is both boring and homogeneous. This can be summed up neatly with the sentiment, "What's next—*Pez: The Movie*?"

### » 2. Steven Spielberg and George Lucas

Though dissing Spielberg is generally not considered a career move, it's a widely held belief that *Jaws* and *Star Wars* and/or a combination thereof can be held responsible for shifting the focus on films from artistry to box office. These films were the first instances of what would eventually lead to Talmudic scrutiny of opening nights and per-screen averages. Today, a star can receive no greater accolade than being named as someone who can "open a movie." Julia Roberts and Mel Gibson can "open"; Jessica Lange and William Hurt cannot.

## Take Issue with the MPAA

The MPAA (Motion Picture Association of America) is the ratings body that not even a mother could love, as it is *arbitrary* in its findings, validates Violence over Sex, and wields a more bizarre power than the Foreign Press Association.[9] A never-ending source of mystery and humor is what exactly goes on during the MPAA screenings... "Wait a minute, that breast was up there for thirty-seven seconds, we told them they could only show it for thirty-six."

## Independent Film

Accept that there is no iron-clad definition for Independent Film.

### Know These Three Moments in Independent Film History

1. Steven Soderbergh's *sex, lies and videotape* (1989) debuts at Sundance and launches the modern era of independent filmmaking. The American mainstream sits up and takes notice of this thing called "intelligent filmmaking" conducted outside of the studio system.

2. Quentin Tarantino's *Pulp Fiction* (1994) smashes through the $100 million barrier and shows that not only can independent film be profitable, it can be *highly* profitable.

3. *The Blair Witch Project* (1999), made for less money than it costs to create a thirty-second television spot, turns the entire movie business upside down with a clever marketing plan leveraging the Internet and managing to scare the bejeezus out of the movie studios, who suddenly feel that they might become obsolete.

---

9. The Foreign Press Association is the group that votes on the Golden Globes every year.

---

### » *A Narrative Trope*

*Be cognizant that* Pulp Fiction *owes a debt of narrative gratitude to what can be called "that* Rashomon *thing." Long before Quentin Tarantino ever rented his first video, filmmaker Akira Kurosawa had twisted story logic on its head with his landmark film* Rashomon *based on a Ryunosuke Alutagawa short story. In that movie Kurosawa broke new ground, telling the tale of a murdered samurai from seven different points of view. A narrative trope, which over time, has come to be viewed as a "Rashomon."*

---

### » *On Set*

Best Boy—Assistant to Key Grip and Gaffer

Key Grip—The Handyman

The Gaffer—If you think your friends are handy with the duct tape, you should see what this guy can do. Generally fixes the lights. The head electrician.

Director of Photography (DP)—Makes sure the Look, Mood, and Feel of the film are right. (When you see a director huddled with somebody in a black-and-white publicity still, it is probably the DP.) Synonymous with Cinematographer.

---

## Oh, Those French

Foreign cinema has a cachet similar to that of independent film, as they both play in what is commonly referred to as art-house theaters. The French, wanting to reclaim cinema for the people,[10] launched the Nouvelle Vague or New Wave at the end of the fifties. Made up of a bunch of writers for *Cahiers du Cinema*,[11] they chose to make "personal" films or, more accurately, anti-establishment films that had individual style. The mack daddy of the genre is Jean-Luc Godard's *A Bout de Souffle*, a film that exhibits a terrific kind of frenetic energy and shows unabashed enthusiasm for filmmaking. In the same way that Neil Young is the godfather of grunge, Godard is the godfather of jump-cut, freaked-out hand-held,[12] home-made-looking movies.

---

10. In 1789 they wanted to reclaim the state. In the 1940s Jean-Paul Sartre wanted to reclaim individuality and personal responsibility, and in the 1980s they have been very busy reclaiming fashion.
11. *Cahiers du Cinema*—a magazine devoted to Cinema as Art. Pronunciation is KAI-yay doo SIN-a-muh.
12. In more recent years the hand-held camera has been used to great effect on TV. The herky-jerky motion of the hand-held camera reentered American consciousness with the crazed first airings of *NYPD Blue*. The next great use of it was indeed in cinema when Woody Allen shot *Husbands and Wives*, which had so many cuts and pans people were nearly induced to vomit. The latest and perhaps most effective use of the hand-held is the 1999 monster hit *The Blair Witch Project*, a film so dizzyingly shot that people did indeed experience motion sickness.

## Some Lines That Will Make You Laugh, Cry, and Do It All Over Again

You know those lines in movies that are so perfect that you say to yourself, Save that. Well, here are a few, and a possible setting for each.

On Smell, Victory, and Waking Up
"I love the smell of napalm in the morning."
—Robert Duvall in *Apocalypse Now*

On Presidential Politics, Mating, Dating, and Life
"There can be only one."
—Christopher Lambert in *The Highlander*

On Boyhood Futures, and Post-Graduate Studies
"I just want to say one word to you—just one word: 'Plastics.'"
—A party guest to Dustin Hoffman in *The Graduate*
(Today one could substitute the following words: Internet, convergence broadband.)

On the State of the Union, Your Job, Your Relationship
"I'm mad as hell and I'm not going to take this anymore."
—Crazed network anchor Peter Finch in *Network*

On Knowing When to Say When
"A man's got to know his limitations."
—Clint Eastwood in *Magnum Force*

On Vanity
"All right, Mr. De Mille. I'm ready for my closeup."
—Gloria Swanson in *Sunset Blvd.*

On What Goes Well with Chianti
"A census taker once tried to test me. I ate his liver with some fava beans and a nice Chianti."
—Anthony Hopkins in *The Silence of the Lambs*

# CELLULOID HEROES

On the Difference between Folks
(Can Be Applied to the Chasm between the Sexes)
 "What we've got here is a failure to communicate."
 —Strother Martin in *Cool Hand Luke*

On Being Sexy
 "I'm not bad, I'm just drawn that way."
 —Jessica Rabbit in *Who Framed Roger Rabbit*

On Doing Things Just Because
 "If you build it, they will come." —The Voice in *Field of Dreams*

On How to Dodge Bullets in Latin American Countries
 "Serpentine, Shelly, Serpentine." —Peter Falk in *The In-Laws*

On the Likelihood of Meeting with Defeat
 "Inconceivable!"
 —Wallace Shawn (with a lisp) in *The Princess Bride*

On Being Accommodating
 "As you wish." —Wesley in *The Princess Bride*

On Being Seduced
 "Mrs. Robinson, you're trying to seduce me, aren't you?"
 —Dustin Hoffman in *The Graduate*

On Being Committed to Achieving a Goal
 "We're on a mission from God."
 —Dan Aykroyd in *The Blues Brothers*

On Being Worried
 "Is it safe?" —Laurence Olivier in *Marathon Man*

On the Perfect State of Mind
 "It's like seventy degrees all the time."
 —From the Kids in the Hall film *Brain Candy*

# Required Reading: The Hollywood Biography

The Hollywood memoir or tell-all has one simple premise, which is: I-was-right-and-everybody-else-was wrong-and-I-never-got-the-credit-I-deserved-but-that's-the-way-it-goes-because-Hollywood-is-a-small,-petty,-venal place. Here are the top three candidates in this vein.

| AUTHOR | BOOK | FILMS | OUTLANDISH CLAIM |
|---|---|---|---|
| Julia Phillips | *You'll Never Eat Lunch in This Town Again* | *Taxi Driver* *The Sting* *Close Encounters of the Third Kind* | That under the pretense that a producer should and would do anything in order to get a picture made she kissed a young Steven Spielberg with tongue to keep him motivated during *Close Encounters*. |
| Robert Evans | *The Kid Stays in the Picture* | *Chinatown* *Godfather*[13] *The Cotton Club* *Marathon Man* | That in the depths of a horrific coke binge he advised Henry Kissinger as to how to handle the possible fall-out from Watergate. |

---

13. Though uncredited, Evans claims it was he who had Coppola go in and re-edit the picture to restore it to its original three-hour-opus status.

| AUTHOR | BOOK | FILMS | OUTLANDISH CLAIM |
|---|---|---|---|
| Jane Hamsher | *Killer Instinct* | *Natural Born Killers* | That Oliver Stone did mushrooms—gasp! And that Quentin Tarantino behaved like a childish weenie in his efforts to prevent her and her partner from making the film.[14] |

## The Last Shot of the Day

The final shot of the day on a movie set is called the Martini.

---

14. The book details the neuroses and drug intake of Mr. Stone and the emotional inadequacies of Mr. Tarantino to such a degree that when Mr. Tarantino ran into one of the principals in the book in a Los Angeles eatery, Mr. Tarantino promptly "bitch-slapped" said principal. Mr. Harvey Weinstein of Miramax fame brokered the peace, and the story has now become a part of Hollywood legend.

# Linguistic Interlude IV: Yiddish

*You never know when a little Yiddish might go a long way. And it's not necessary to use too thick an accent to play it up; just knowing some of these words is proof of your Judaic literacy.*

» *Macher* (Mah-KHER)
A big shot, as in Billy Joel's "You had to be a big shot." Also *ganzamacher*—a very big shot. Useful for letting other people know if somebody's a big deal: "He's a real ganzamacher."

» *Kvetch* (kuh-vetch)
To complain, to whine. Can also be kvetching.

» *Mishegas* (mish-uh-gahs)
Silliness, craziness of a dizzy kind. "You, you're full of mishegas."

» *Mishpochah* (mish-puh-chuh)
Family. One's people. Following Thanksgiving or other such holidays: "Were you hanging with your mishpochah?"

» *Shiksa* (shih-ksuh)
A non-Jewish female. Most often accompanied by the word *goddess*, as in, "Who's the shiksa goddess?"

» *Shmatte* (Shma-tah)
Rags. Clothes. "What are those shmatte you got on?"
Also, if you are in the fashion or clothing industry, this is a very humble way of sharing your business: "I'm in the shmatte business."

» *Shmendrik* (shmen-drick)
A stupid person. Much more inventive than the more commonly used *putz* and shmuck.

» *Shnorer* (shnorr-er)
A leech, a mooch, a hanger-on. One who leads a better quality of life by attaching himself parasitically to good situations.

» *Shvitz* (shvitz)
To sweat or to take a steam bath. When going to go work out: "I've got to go shvitz."

» *Yente* (Yen-tuh)
A busybody.

» *Zay gezunt* (Zai-guh-zoont)
Yiddish equivalent of "Live Long and Prosper."

# TELEVISION: THE DRUG OF A NATION[1]

"Art is a moral passion married to entertainment.

Moral passion without enter-

tainment is propaganda, and

entertainment without moral

passion is television."

—Emma Thompson, from

*The Sense & Sensibility Screenplay & Diaries*

---

1. Taken from the song by the Disposable Heroes of Hiphoprisy wherein lead singer Michael Franti refers to the TV as "the methadone metronome," "the cathode ray nipple," and suggests that "the mothers of our nation should remind us that we are sitting too close to . . . the Television."

> *Creepy Facts about Our TV Culture . . .*

*Over 98 percent of American homes have a TV.[2] The average American female watches 4 1/2 hours of TV a day. The average American male watches 4 hours of TV a day.*

## Suggested Attitude You Should Publicly Affect Toward Television

Although TV has become an essential luxury, it remains advisable to maintain a healthy disdain for the so-called idiot box. For steering away from note-by-note recitations of favorite shows, not letting on that your life revolves around TV, and holding back testimonials on the depth of the void in your life once Seinfeld ended tends to suggest that you might have other, more enlightening leisure-time pursuits.

## The Early Early Days

> Factoid: Who Invented TV

Philo T. Farnsworth of Rigby, Idaho, invented the TV as we know it. As the story goes, he drew a diagram for his idea of a TV on the blackboard when he was fourteen years old. In 1927, at the age of twenty-one, he transmitted the first electronic TV picture. Attempts were made to steal the idea, attempts that he fought tooth-and-nail and against which he triumphed, only to end up an embittered alcoholic. Philo, we and the billion-plus *Baywatch* viewers around the world salute you.

---

2. © 1999, Television Bureau of Advertising.

# Members of TV's Golden Age Cast of Characters

## » David Sarnoff and NBC

David Sarnoff inaugurated the modern era of TV with a broadcast at the World's Fair in 1939. He put the peacock in NBC's "proud as a peacock" by pioneering the use of color.

## » Bill Paley and CBS

Paley created the modern TV network with CBS. He signed up Lucille Ball, Jackie Gleason, Ed Sullivan, and Mary Tyler Moore to do TV shows, and was a strong supporter of Mr. News—Edward R. Murrow. He put the Tiffany in the Tiffany Network.

## » Milton Berle

Milton Berle, or "Uncle Miltie," was "Mr. Television," giving the world the first real TV hit ever, *Texaco Star Theater*. Legend also has it that he is possessed of the largest package ever. Consider both the former and the latter in much the same way you do state capitals or the first ten digits of $\pi$, necessary but rarely invoked.

# TV Programming

# Programming Geniuses 101

Once upon a time, programming a TV network was the boyhood dream of millions of media-savvy, stardust-craving youth. Here are three geniuses who put their *imprimatur* on network scheduling and their respective claims to fame.

## » Barry Diller

Programming Overlord:

- He launched the Fox network, bringing the world *The Simpsons* and game shows like *Studs*.
- He bought QVC and made buying cubic zirconia from the comfort of your own couch a reality.
- He is the man who invented the TV Movie aka the Movie of the Week.
- Currently turning perennial also-ran USA Networks into an Internet/TV empire for the new millennium.

---

## » *The Number One Big Kahuna Is John Malone*

*John Malone is the most powerful person in the history of Cable TV (yes, more powerful than Ted Turner). Malone's company, TCI, which he sold to AT&T in 1998 for $54 billion, was at the time the largest cable company in the United States. His company, Liberty, is the largest shareholder in Time Warner, second largest in Rupert Murdoch's NewsCorp (after Rupert himself). He has a major piece of the following channels: The Discovery Channel, Fox Sports, F/X, The Home Shopping Network, BET, and E!*

*In short, no matter what anybody says about cable or digital TV, Internet convergence and broadband, you can reply, "I wouldn't bet against John Malone."*

---

## » Fred Silverman

The only person, to date, to program CBS, ABC, and NBC. He made the TV programming world safe for *Charlie's Angels, Mork and Mindy, Laverne and Shirley,* and *The Bionic Woman.*

Claim to Fame: Silverman put *Roots* on eight nights in a row—something that had never been done previously, except with events such as the Olympics.

## » Brandon Tartikoff

Took NBC from worst to first. (Employ the phrase "worst to first" whenever possible—it works equally in sports, finance, and class rankings.) Tartikoff remains the prototype wunderkind of the TV world, running NBC by the age of thirty-five.

Claim to Fame: Legendary idea man who gave good memo.

In urging Stephen J. Cannell to create the *A-Team*: "*Road Warrior, Magnificent Seven, Dirty Dozen, Mission: Impossible* all rolled into one, and Mr. T drives the car."

A suggestion to Bill Cosby on what would be a good TV show: "A black *Family Ties.*"

And his most famous two-word synopsis: "MTV Cops." (Also known as *Miami Vice.*)

## The Development Process

1. A writer creates a show, and said writer pitches said show to a network. In said pitch he says something like "It's a vampire family show; think *Buffy* meets *Family Ties*" or "It's a surreal espionage show fronted by a hot new band with supernatural powers. Think *X-Files* meets *The Man from Uncle* with *The Monkees* thrown in."

2. The network, thrilled by the writer's ideas but possibly alarmed by certain aspects that might not appeal to the masses—aka the lowest common denominator—gives the writer *notes.*

3. The writer reviews the network's notes, taking into account their comments about *story arc* and *character development,* ignoring their comments on *sexuality,* but heeding their desire to move the show from Puerto Rico to Connecticut.

4. The writer pitches the show anew.

5. The network buys the pitch, but reserves the right to make certain changes to the program should they so desire.

6. The writer pens a pilot.

7. The network gives the writer *notes* on the pilot and suggests some minor character changes. As the network is skewing for a younger demographic, perhaps instead of having the show be about five men and three women all over the age of forty-five dealing with real-life issues of death, disease, and marital infidelity, they may recommend that the show be set in a high-school or even junior-high environment and focus more on the trials and tribulations of getting good grades, being popular, and, if it really has to be there, cheating on the boyfriend.

8. The writer listens to the network notes. Readjusts the age and gender mix as requested and resubmits the script.

9. The network approves the pilot.

10. The pilot is shot with the hopes that it will double as the series premier.

11. The network sees the pilot and shelves it, but expresses interest in the "general idea of what is going on." Asks the writer to write a new script for the series.

In a best-case scenario, following the screening of the pilot, the network commits to the number of episodes they would like to see. That number (hopefully being at least thirteen, possibly being as many as twenty-two, but sometimes being as few as six) is placed and "production" begins.

## » But What's the Goal?

The Goal in series television is to get to syndication. This means making it to 100 half-hours (actual running time of twenty-two minutes). Syndication is television sitcom heaven. So when you can't understand how a show can possibly still be on the air, know that it stays alive in order to get that crucial one-hundredth episode in order to collect those all-important syndication dollars.

## The TV Drama

On television there are the dramas: legal, medical, ensemble, detective, mystery, cop, family, adult, action, teen, and soap. Three creators and the works they gave us . . .

## » Aaron Spelling

Likes to be called Mister, period. Not Mister Spelling. Not Mister Aaron—just Mister. He is the reigning world champ of television programming. Check *Guinness*—he's there.

Like a good TV show, his career comes in three tidy acts.

Act I    He gives the world hipster cop dramas: *The Mod Squad, The Rookies, S.W.A.T., Starsky and Hutch.*

Act II    He gives the world jiggle TV: *Charlie's Angels, The Love Boat, Fantasy Island,* and defines a certain kind of high-end bitch cat-fight with *Dynasty.*

Act III    He delivers unto us *Beverly Hills 90210, Melrose Place,* and *Models Inc.* (Oh, and Tori too.)

---

## » Starsky and Hutch *and That Whole TV Violence Thing*

Starsky and Hutch *launched the first "Does it imitate us or do we imitate it?" debate regarding violence on TV. The number of people being killed on S&H was rather high, and it all occurred in graphic fashion.*

*This is handy for that moment when the inevitable office shooting occurs and everybody starts talking about the deplorable state of media today—you can be the one to say, "Hey, we've been talking about this since the days of* Starsky and Hutch."

## » David E. Kelley

The TV world's Alpha Male. Creator of *Ally McBeal, The Practice, Picket Fences,* and *Chicago Hope.*

And he writes all shows himself—in longhand—between the hours of nine and five. Then goes home to his wife, Michelle Pfeiffer. And he went to Princeton. And he was captain of the ice hockey team. And he's a lawyer.

## » Steven Bochco

Boundary pusher extraordinaire. Creator of *NYPD Blue, Hill Street Blues, L.A. Law, Murder One,* and a wonderful police musical, *Cop Rock.* Yes, singing, dancing cops.

The Log-Line on Bochco: He made network TV safe for Dennis Franz's naked butt and the use of the word *scumbag.*

# The TV Comedy

There are numerous varieties of comedies: family, sophisticated, young adult, children, workplace, and that whole white-people-in-New York-who-seem-to-have-incredible-apartments-without-having-incredible-jobs-trust-funds-or-wealthy-significant-others genre.

## Three Giants of the TV Comedy World: For Better or for Worse

### » The Old School: Norman Lear

The wise master of the sophisticated sitcom. Norman Lear gave the world comedy as bitter pill, as depicted in

> ## » *The Q Rating*
>
> *There are the Nielsens and there is the Q rating. It's a rating that says how popular a TV star is with the American public. It's a subjective measurement that is found by polling average households. Its influence can lead to programming decisions that at first brush may seem strange. A great example from the eighties, one that might explain one of the more peculiar phenomena in TV history, is that Urkel, geek-boy from* Family Matters, *had a Q rating that was off the charts.*

*All in the Family, Maude,* and *The Jeffersons.* Gave the world "Meathead" as a derisive term of endearment, and provided the world with its first upscale black sitcom with *The Jeffersons.*

## » The Most Successful School: Carsey Werner

Carsey Werner is the production company that gave birth to *The Cosby Show, Roseanne,* and *Third Rock from the Sun.* What to do for an encore having created one of the most successful production companies ever? Go ahead and create your own network with the help of Oprah and Geraldine "Gerry" Laybourne, the former head of Nickelodeon.

## » The Saccharine School: Miller Boyett

Miller Boyett is a production company that has their very own circle of Hell reserved for them.[3] They are responsible for foisting the Olsen twins upon an unsuspecting nation (*Full House*), giving birth to the TV

---

3. See "Literature for the Lazy" for Dante's nine circles of hell.

phenomenon called Urkel (*Family Matters*), and having a lead character called Balki (*Perfect Strangers*). Wildly successful, but working for them is considered a kind of necessary purgatory for the aspiring TV writer.

The Insider Nod: If a friend utters something so disgustingly cute as to border on saccharine, the TV-literate thing to say would be "Keep that up and they'll have you writing for Miller Boyett shows."

## Nominal Comments on Programming

### "*The Simpsons* Is the Most Important Television Show of the Past 25 Years."

In a medium where freshness and originality are the first casualties of success, *The Simpsons*' reference-a-minute mania gives those wacky Harvard[4] boys an opportunity to riff on everything from Botticelli[5] to *The Birds*[6] and from Samuel Johnson[7] to Scooby Doo.[8] The result is an animated half-hour program that can be viewed as the quintessential post-modern pop-culture fantasia. And you can challenge anyone in the room to name something more continually innovative, groundbreaking, and just plain funny.

---

4. The Harvard Mafia rules the comedy roost of Hollywood. The highest profile member of the Mafia was, at the time of the writing of this book, Conan O'Brien.
5. "The Last Temptation of Homer."
6. "Bart the Mother."
7. "Bart Gets an F."
8. "Krusty Gets Busted."

Three Shows about Which You Can Say, "The Only Thing That Kept Me Alive during the 90s Was . . ."

In the early nineties, as the nation awoke from the great cultural desert of the previous decade, three clever, funny, and fringe comedy shows broke out of the pack. Here's a guide to where you might want to position yourself if you were to triangulate wit, show-biz acumen, and cross-dressing.

» If You Aspire to Be a Lover of Post–Monty Python Sketch-Comedy Genius:

*"The only thing that kept me alive during the nineties was the* Kids in the Hall."

Talk about how the Kids, as they were known, were raucously brilliant, incredibly funny, and just a wee bit too "in drag" for mass acceptance by the American public. Liking the Kids shows that you are:

a.    comfortable with your sexuality;
b.    know of sketch comedy troupes beyond *Saturday Night Live*;
c.    don't have a grudge against Canadians.

» If You're Someone Who Yearns for Johnny Carson Even if You Never Watched Him:

*"The only thing that kept me alive during the early nineties was* Larry Sanders."

You can remark on how *The Larry Sanders Show* was criminally funny, redefined intelligent comedy humor while skewering the entire late-night genre—making the most of the fever pitch of the Late-Night wars between Leno and Letterman.

The lover of *Larry Sanders* appreciates the irony of insider entertainment jokes, was able to afford Cable TV in the early nineties, and is something of a misanthrope.

Suggest that if you could be anybody in the world it would be Rip Torn's character Artie, the show runner.

## » If You're a Person Who Specializes in Loving That Rare and Obscure Thing:

*"The only thing that kept me alive in the nineties was* The Ben Stiller Show."

To give that elusive yet informed impression, much like the guy who enjoys late-model cars that cost more in maintenance than the original purchase price, claim allegiance to early Ben Stiller. From his early days on MTV to a full (more or less) run of thirteen episodes on Fox, Stiller skewered TV, Film, and Music in a knowing, slapstick vein. It was the launching ground for cutesy favorite Janeane Garofalo, maniac freak Andy Dick, and Bob Odenkirk—the other half of Bob and David from *Mr. Show.*

From his stereotypical agent with the headset to his dead-on Bono imitation to the parodies of *90210, The Ben Stiller Show* lives on in hearts of media-savvy nerds everywhere.

# A Few Obvious Targets to Blame for the Decline of Western Civilization

## Obvious Target: *Entertainment Tonight*

What:

From the ingratiating theme song[9] to the lavish seven-minute stories that begin with "Here we are on a beach in Maui with the Hawaiian Tropic Swimsuit Team," the media apocalypse can be traced directly to the debut of *Entertainment Tonight* on September 14, 1981.

How To: Suggest freely that "*Entertainment Tonight* is single-handedly responsible for the triumph of style over substance in the field of endeavor once known as TV journalism."

## Strangely Addictive Guilty Pleasure Target: *The Real World*

What:

The MTV show wherein five to seven strategically chosen heterogeneous people made up of a calculatedly desirable mix of gay, straight, boy, girl, Caucasian, Asian, and African-American agree to disagree publicly over a six-month period and have the whole experience filmed.

How-To: Blame *The Real World* for suggesting to the whole of America, if not the world, that it is telegenic. Complain openly that only through the use of quick-cutting, and high-powered, upbeat sound tracks could the lives of average people with marginal attention spans

---

9. In keeping with the notion that all things in life have been referred to in a *Seinfeld* episode, recall if you will the show where Kramer would suffer a near epileptic seizure when he heard Mary Hart's voice from *Entertainment Tonight*.

> » *Three Seminal Moments*
> *in Talk-Show History*
>
> *Phil Donahue Wears a Dress*
>
> *Jenny Jones Guest Is Embarrassed on*
> *National TV by Gay Crush*
>
> *Geraldo's Nose Is Broken during an*
> *Onstage Brawl Featuring Nazis*

> » *When All Else Fails, Dream*
> *Up Talk-Show Categories*
>
> *For example:*
>
> *Women Who Love Men with Big Options Packages*
> *but Don't Know What Fork to Use for Their Oysters*
>
> *Women Who Use Their Cell Phones in*
> *Grocery Stores and the Men Who Call Them*
>
> *Men Who Eat Out of the Bulk Food Bins and*
> *the Store Managers Who Catch Them*

be transformed into shining media icons of the end of the century. (And while you're at it, admit that your favorite episodes are the shows where they screen all the videos for tryouts.)

## Less Obvious, More Insidious Target: CNBC

What:

Up-to-the-minute financials being reported on by clever talking heads boosted by production values previously reserved for stories of earth-shaking import. "AOL down two and three-eighths—here from the trading floor the News Live!" This channel and its cousin CNNFN have succeeded in making the formerly mundane business of counting money seem exciting, compelling, and even sexy.

How-To: Nations of cube and office dwellers are now so completely attuned to the most minute fluctuations in the economy and their "positions" that they are no longer able to focus on what they were doing in the first place.

Upshot: Legions of folks talking about "the Brain," the Squawk Box, and developing advanced ADD by flipping among their stock ticker, the TV, and the phone to make calls to their broker.

## I Saw It on the Evening News: From Kennedy to Kennedy

### Critical Moments That Shaped TV News

Here are five key moments that have stretched the boundaries of live coverage. (For space purposes, no shotguns to the head, car chases aside from O.J., or self-immolation have been listed.)

### » The Kennedy Campaign

Jack Kennedy ushered in the modern TV era, winning his campaign with a combination of charm, good looks, and clever repartee, and outshining challenger Richard Milhous Nixon in head-to-head televised debates.

In retrospect it seems unfair even to think of putting Nixon and Kennedy side by side in front of a TV camera. Even now, thirty-five years after the fact, Kennedy's image burns brightly while Nixon's remains synonymous with deceit, defeat, and a dog named Checkers!

What It's Done to the Political System: Not just the Kennedy-Nixon debates but Kennedy's entire tenure placed an emphasis on style over substance (who can forget all those adorable home movies) that has devolved into "sound-bite politics" spoon-fed to attention-deficit TV voters.

## » Lee Harvey Oswald

Lee Harvey Oswald was gunned down, live, on national television by Jack Ruby. No fancy car chase, no public showdown. He was mowed down in cold blood.

How It Influenced TV Viewing: In some weird, small, twisted way, Americans have been glued to their sets ever since; maybe they just might see something like it again.

## » The Gulf War

The TV war that put the Cable News Network (CNN) on the map. Before the Gulf War, CNN was just some crazy little outfit that some guy named Turner was trying to foist upon an unsuspecting American public. After the Gulf War and the American-army-sanctioned coverage—of shriek missiles and up-to-the-minute strike footage—CNN was a force to be reckoned with.

What It's Done for War: Gave everybody a quick, snappy comment whenever a war breaks out: "Hey, wonder if CNN's ratings will go up."

## » The Chase

Following O.J. over the freeways of Los Angeles and through the hearts of America. The most bizarre news coverage in the history of Television wound up being a mere prelude to the several-month-long insanity of the trial that would follow. Who can forget those exquisitely weird moments when O.J. was making what appeared to be his final end run, fans cheering him on with placards saying GO JUICE GO?

What It Meant to the Viewer: One of the most surreal viewing experiences possible. The equivalent, in some ways, of the Kennedy assassination for a nation of TV watchers. Ask anyone where they were during the Chase and they'll be able to tell you time, place, and emotion. (Not including the annoyed NBA fans who were pissed to be missing the playoffs.)

## » Columbine

Columbine reporting was an apex of questionable journalism. It's one thing to have live coverage of teenagers crying as they emerge from their high school battleground, but to track them down after the fact is another low altogether.

To make the point, relate the following: "I remember watching at one point when they were interviewing a Columbine girl by phone, live from the television studio. And she's talking about her friends, and bawling and how sad it all was and how she's gonna miss them and then realizes she's on TV and she's like, 'How the fuck did you get my number?' and hangs up."

# Insomniac Television

Late-night TV watching, the hours between 2 and 5 A.M., is split up into three component parts: infomercials, seventies movies, and *Columbo*. Have no shame about your love of infomercials; everyone has the urge to buy the wax that lets you take a blowtorch to your car, or the physical-therapy device that will give you abs of steel, or buns of steel, or simply the powerful cleanser you can use on countertops, shower curtains, bathtub drains, and your child's pacifier. It's only human. Talk about it. Others will share your pain.

## » The Importance of *Columbo*

You get to see all those guest stars in full mid-seventies form: John Cassavetes, Johnny Cash, Robert Culp, Ricardo Montalban, and even Leonard Nimoy.

You get to transfer all of your annoyance at not sleeping directly to Columbo as he literally pesters the killer(s) to such a degree that they would rather confess than hear, "Oh, and one more thing..." (This is a tactic that can and will prove effective when interrogating a colleague, boss, or friend. However, with intimates "Oh, and one more thing . . ." this line of attack can escalate a tiff into a war, a war into a breakup, and a breakup into never speaking again.)

The slow, methodical fashion in which the crimes are solved allows you, the half-awake, blurry-visioned viewer, to actually piece together the crime along with Columbo—giving you an odd sense of satisfaction just as you realize that yet again you got only three hours of sleep before the big presentation.

## TV Catchphrase Hall of Fame

» Seinfeld

In its own inimitable way, *Seinfeld* introduced several phrases and concepts into the vernacular. Some choice ones:

*Not That There's Anything Wrong with That*—Cousin to the generic "His heart is in the right place." A fine way to say the following, "I don't necessarily participate in a certain kind of activity, and while I don't condone it, I don't really condemn it either. But I sort of do think it's odd." (The episode wherein it is thought that perhaps George and Jerry might be, um, y'know...)

*Master of My Domain*—In what was arguably the most famous episode ever, one dedicated to the pursuit of pleasuring one-self, otherwise known as onanism. This episode was actually dedicated to *not* pleasuring oneself. This phrase, meaning "I did not pleasure myself," was introduced to the American culture at large. It is a nudge-nudge, wink-wink kind of thing.

*Shrinkage*—Here the *Seinfeld* folks introduced into the greater culture a way to describe the side-effect of cold water upon *Homo sapiens'* male equipment. Shrinkage is a fine thing to throw around at pool parties, lake parties, beach bonfires, and in high-country rivers—especially if skinny-dipping is involved.

*Worlds Collide*—Intoned by George when his fiancée, Susan, started spending more time with Elaine. The safe-couple world of George and Susan was put on a collision course with the self-obsessed world of George, Jerry, Elaine, and Kramer. Invoking the proper hysterical mania, *"Worlds collide!"* lends this phrase greater credibility.

Appropriate times to voice this: girlfriend wanting to meet parents arriving in town; girlfriend expressing desire to meet old girlfriend; girlfriend wanting to go on bachelor-party weekend to Vegas—you get the idea. Invoking the "worlds collide" terminology raises the stakes to interplanetary disaster—it's a safe way to avoid letting someone know you really just don't want to be seen with them in public.

*Close Talker*—This is more of a concept than a phrase. But the notion of a "close talker" opens up a whole series of *Seinfeld*s and is a funny way to reference anyone who feels a desire to get in your face when they're speaking to you.

## » Cop Shows

*And Hey, Let's Be Careful Out There*—This came from the *Hill Street Blues* watch commander every morning before he sent his crews out to deal with the scum of the earth. It is a fine parting comment to anyone going off on a journey, large or small, treacherous or safe. It goes something like this: A person approaches a threshold—car door, home, office space—to exit, you say just at the moment their back is turning away, "And hey"—they turn three-quarters of the way back to you—"let's be careful out there."

*Book 'im Danno*—from *Hawaii Five-O*. It's just rare that you have an opportunity to use it.

## » Sci-Fi Geekdom

*Live Long and Prosper*—From *Star Trek*. Geek for *"Ciao!"* "Bye," *"Au revoir!"* etc. If possible, place the index and middle finger together, the third and fourth together, and make a V.

*Make It So*—From *Star Trek: The Next Generation*. Geek for "Dude, hook me up." When you require a friend to do you a solid. "Make it so," adding "Number One"—for that is how Picard refers to his first officer—is optional.

# Everything I Ever Learned Was from TV Theme Songs

Allow the stored-up vast knowledge of TV themes to rightly serve as a reservoir of knowledge from which you can dispense advice to loved ones and colleagues alike.

## On the Wisdom of Committing an Illicit Act

"Don't do the crime,
   If you can't do the time.
   No, no don't do it."

—From *Baretta*

## For That Seventies Motivational Feel

"There's a new girl in town and she's feeling good!"
—From *Alice*

## On Seeing Someone Freshly Out of Surgery

Stage direction: *Hand cupped over mouth*
"Steve Austin, a man barely alive . . .
   We have the technology
   We can rebuild him. . . ."
—From the *Six Million Dollar Man*

We Interrupt This Chapter to Bring You
the Following Commercial Announcement:
The Most Important Television Advertisement Ever

1984: Macintosh.
Designed by Jay Chiat of the Chiat-Day
ad agency.

The Moment:
Halftime at the Super Bowl, 1984. On-screen, an
Orwellian world of gray, dreary obedience. A
lone blond woman in red shorts and a white top
is seen running with an oversized hammer. She's
running, running, running toward something.
She's running away from something. She enters
a room filled with obedient information drones
staring at the Leader on-screen. She hurls the
hammer. Forces are converging upon her. She
shatters the screen. Apple Macintosh. A revolution is born.

## » *The Best TV Sign-Off Ever*

*David Brinkley had pretty much resigned completely.
Before he did, he managed to say the following things
on air. "Among things I admire, almost near the top is
creativeness. . . . Bill Clinton has none of it. He has not a
creative bone in his body. Therefore he's a bore, and will
always be a bore."*

# The Best End to a TV Show Ever

TV shows come and TV shows go. Every season they go
on summer hiatus so the industry's youth can go off to
begin major-motion-picture careers and senior members can go to Tuscany. And whether it is a seasonal
farewell or the final curtain, either way it's a good time to
talk about Bob Newhart's final show.

For a period of time the balding and occasionally
funny man known as Bob Newhart played a Vermont
innkeeper on national TV. This, his second major series,
followed his extraordinary first series, where he played a
balding and occasionally funny psychologist married to
the relentlessly perky and good-natured Suzanne
Pleshette.

Well, as all shows do, this latter show, the one where
the balding and occasionally funny man known as Bob
Newhart played a Vermont innkeeper, reached its final
season. The finale was shrouded in secrecy. Nobody
knew how the show was going to end, not even the crew
shooting the final episode.

Bob the innkeeper gets whacked by a golf ball. He's
shown waking up in bed next to . . . Suzanne Pleshette,
his TV wife from the first series. He turns to her and
says, "Honey I just had the strangest dream. I was an
innkeeper in Vermont for eight years. And I wasn't married to you."

## Words to Part By

"Good night, John Boy."
—From *The Waltons*

# Linguistic Interlude V: English

*Big words for people who want to sound big.*

*Gravitas* (grah-vee-tahs)
Weight, bearing, stature.

*Jejune* (ja-jhoon)
Insipid, weak, or dull. One step past sophomoric. A way to refer to a film, cartoon, or the actions of a drunken friend who is insisting on being childlike.

*Miscegenation* (miss-eg-un-nay-shun)
Sex between races.

*Mores* (mor-ays)
The social/moral code of your people. Usually invoked when such codes are in danger of being violated or have recently been violated.

*Obfuscate* (ob-fyoo-skayt)
To confuse or becloud; to render indistinct.

*Peccadillo* (pek-uh-dill-oh)
Something slightly sinful or indulgent that could be forgiven.

*Pedantic* (puh-dant-ick)
Having the character of being too preachy in an academic sense of the word.

*Prodigal* (prod-ih-guhl)
Recklessly extravagant.

*Pulchritude* (pul-kri-tood)
Physical beauty and appeal. Also pulchritudinous.

*Pusillanimous* (pyoo-suh-layn-uh-mus)
Lacking courage, as in the Lion in *The Wizard of Oz*.

# Ooh, Baby, Baby, It's a Wired World. . . .[1]

"Every day computers
are making people easier
to use."

—Subhead of Silicon Valley
subversive magazine,
*In Formation*

---

1. With apologies to Cat Stevens; though, as he became a
   militant Muslim who felt "Salman Rushdie must die," the
   score may now be even.

## The Importance of Geek

Remember that scene in *Airplane* with the two black dudes talking jive? One's hurting bad and the stewardess can't help him out because she is simply not down with his dialect.[2] And a little old lady[3] sitting nearby leans in and says, "Oh, Stewardess—I speak jive."

The spirit of this chapter is the same, though instead of being about "jive-talking," the goal is to allow you to feel as if you can safely say, "I speak 'geek.'" For in the dot.com era, it's become something of a necessity to know the difference between a byte and a baud, bandwidth and bandwagon, and silicon and silicone.[4]

## But First a Word about the Personal Computer

Before the World Wide Web, before the Internet, there was the Personal Computer or PC. The mythology surrounding its birth and arrival in America's homes, like many a good epic tale, is marked by legend and apocrypha, some of which is amusing, some of which is marked by intrigue and personal betrayal, and still other parts of which are just plain boring.

---

2. Neither does the audience, as subtitles are present in this seminal piece of early-eighties culture.
3. The little old lady happens to be Barbara Billingsley, better known as Beaver's Mom from the classic fifties sitcom and the classic late-eighties exercise in irony, *Leave It to Beaver.*
4. The smart-ass answer to what's the difference between Silicon and Silicone is "400 miles," the Silicon being Silicon Valley in San Jose, and the Silicone being Silicone Implants, meaning Los Angeles: the distance between them, 400 miles.

# Momentous Milestones on the Road to the PC Revolution

This chapter is focused primarily on the events of the last three decades as opposed to the entire history of "Computing."

## Xerox PARC: 1970

*What It Is:* Xerox opened the Palo Alto Research Center (PARC) to pioneer advances in computer science. It was the ultimate think tank in its day; merely alluding to the PARC era as a golden age in innovation, limitless possibility, and geek chic, all undertaken in a climate of altruism as opposed to avarice, suggests a deep and well-studied understanding of the field of computer development.

*Relevance to You and the People You Love:* Xerox PARC was behind the following developments: the GUI (Graphic User Interface),[5] pronounced Goo-EE; the Mouse; the Laser Printer; and ethernet.[6] And though we take all these things for granted now, the whole "point-and-click" thing came out of this little research project.

*Potential Comment (Vis-à-Vis Any of the Latest Advancements in the Field of Hardware and Software Development):* "Yeah, but can what they're doing really hold a candle to what the folks at PARC did?"

---

5. A GUI is an interface, like Windows, Macintosh, or the current iterations of Internet Explorer and Netscape Navigator. The pretty little icons that you can "drag" around a "desktop" all spring from this early work at PARC.
6. Ethernets connect two computers to each other on a network. They are so named because the guy who came up with it, specifically Bob Metcalfe, thought the early-nine-teenth-century notion of ether being the stuff that fills the air to be a very funny concept. So why not call the thing that connects computers together an ethernet?

# Geek Heroes

## » Alan Turing (1912–1954)

Alan Turing broke the German Enigma code during World War II, was hounded to death for being gay, and (for point-scoring purposes) should be remembered as the Father of Computer Science. After Oscar Wilde, Turing is the second most famous subject of the British Royal Empire to be publicly held accountable for crimes of "gross indecency."[7]

Just One of Turing's Massive Contributions: Turing came up with the Turing Test, which was a simple test to determine whether something was either a human or machine.

In a colloquial vein, should someone be so dimwitted or devoid of those qualities that are generally considered to constitute humanity, you can say, "Would they pass the Turing Test?"[8]

## » Richard P. Feynman (1818–1988)

Feynman is the great jokester, lover, and legend of the math/physics/computer science set. His brilliance in the field of physics was matched only by his sense of

---

7. Rather than go to prison, he allowed himself to be injected with estrogen to neutralize his libido.
8. The Turing Test is as follows: A computer and Person A are hooked up to a machine—what exactly that machine is like is irrelevant—and another human is placed in a room or an area away from the computer and Person A. Picture a game show in the fifties. The computer and Person A are asked a series of questions, their input is filtered through the machine, and if the isolated human cannot tell which is which, then the computer has passed "the Turing Test."

humor and his relentless pranks. Even as he became one of the most senior physicists in the world—first on the Manhattan Project at Los Alamos and then as a tenured professor at Caltech—he never let up with the joking, goofing, and trademark playfulness with which he approached his chosen field. (He is best known for a series of freshman physics lectures that he gave at Caltech. If you meet somebody who studies physics, ask, "How 'bout those Feynman lectures?")
Other Notes:

He won the Nobel prize. He wrote a very funny autobiography called *Surely You're Joking, Mr. Feynman.* He is the personal hero of Matt Stone.[9]

Why Feynman:

When seeking a role model or a certain kind of renaissance guy, Feynman is the man. Feynman played the bongos. Feynman taught himself Portuguese. Feynman taught himself how to decipher Mayan hieroglyphics. Feynman is the guy in the Apple "Think Different" campaign whom nobody recognizes.[10]
Anecdotally Speaking:

The Feynman story to abuse freely, one that shows both his humor and his genius, is the following: When Feynman was working at Los Alamos he

---

9. For those people who care about this level of minutiae, Matt Stone is a co-creator of *South Park*. While it may seem to be discursive and something of a non sequitur, this kind of stacking the deck—Feynman is this, Feynman is that, and he's the personal hero of Matt Stone—may render you invincible in a conversation.
10. Another famous scientist who is not generally recognized by the public at large and is in the Apple "Think Different" campaign is R. Buckminster Fuller.

would occasionally crack the combination safes that held secrets of national security—plutoniun production schedules, neutron radiation data, etc. After cracking the safe he would leave a note: "I borrowed document LA4312—Feynman the Safecracker."

## Atari and Baby Steps: 1972

*Why Atari*: In 1972, Steve Jobs went to work for Nolan Bushnell at Atari, the home of the arcade coin-op Pong. You remember Pong? Two paddles and a little blip going back and forth. Jobs recruited his pal Steve Wozniak (later they would go on to found Apple) to work on Breakout, the sequel to Pong.

*Relevance to You*: Atari is, when drawing concentric circles interconnecting the worlds of arcade and home games, home computers and the history of the Silicon Valley, at the very epicenter of all things. Moreover, it serves as a neat cautionary tale as to how *not* to survive in a fast-changing marketplace. They missed out on the Personal Computer, didn't adapt to the changing gaming world, and faded from sight faster than you can say "Bill Gates just earned another 10 million dollars." Bushnell is but one of the many people who looked at Jobs's vision for the personal computer company that would be Apple and said, "Nah."

*Gee-Whiz No-Way Trivia*: Atari is Japanese for the word *checkmate* in the game Go!

## *Popular Electronics* and the MITS Altair 8800: 1975

*Popular Electronics* put the MITS Altair 8800 on its cover in January of 1975. It was hailed as the first "personal computer," and it marked the beginning of the beginning of the beginning of the beginning of *it all*. Paul Allen and Bill Gates, Microsoft's co-founders, made a slimmed-down version of the computer language known as BASIC that ran on the Altair, and the software industry as we know it today was born.

*Relevance to You*: Nearly every story ever having to do with the birth of the PC begins with the day Visionary X (Bill Gates, Paul Allen, Steve Jobs, Steve Wozniak) saw the MITS Altair 8800 on the cover of *Popular Electronics* and experienced a palpable "It's here!" feeling.

*Relevance to People with a Deeper Understanding of Computer Science than You*: The MITS Altair marks the beginning of a geek phenomenon related to their respective earliest experiences with PCs. Beginning with, "Do you remember the MITS Altair?" or its cousin, "What was your first computer?"[11] The computers that people remember with great enthusiasm include but are not limited to: the Commodore Amiga and the Commodore 64, the TRS-80 from Tandy Radio Shack, and the KIM-ONE.

## Apple Computer Is Founded: 1976

Apple Computer was founded on April 1, 1976, by Steve Wozniak and Steve Jobs in a garage. One year later, the Apple II was publicly introduced for $1,295.

---

1. The Internet corollary to this is "How long have you been on-line?" Anyone who answers any date prior to 1990 should be surveyed with great skepticism unless they fit the glasses-and-pocket-protector geek-imaging profile.

Many forget that the reason people originally bought the Apple II was for VisiCalc, an early version of spreadsheet software. Those who do not care about spreadsheets will not care about this bit of historical info. On the other hand, should you be conversing with anyone near the age of forty, he or she will probably recall the arrival of VisiCalc and beam ecstatically at its mention.

*Relevance to You:* Apple revolutionized the field of computing. The Apple mantra, which worked for years, was, "Apple—changing the world one person at a time."

Apple made the world believe in the vision of computers in the home, for the individual, and, depending on which version of revisionist history you are most interested in, may have been completely ripped off by Microsoft when that company came out with Windows.

## IBM, Microsoft, and Q-DOS: 1980

IBM needed an operating system for their soon-to-debut PC, so they turned to Microsoft, who in turn made a call to Tim Paterson of the Seattle Computer Company. Paterson, who had authored something called Q-DOS, for "Quick and Dirty Operating System," sold his program to Microsoft for $50,000.[12]

Microsoft made a few tweaks, called it MS-DOS (MS for Microsoft), and the biggest company in the United States was on its way.

---

12. This particular "Oh-my-God-I-can't-believe-a-corporate-giant-was-erected-upon-the-slim-edifice-of-my-work" can only be surpassed by the sale of the Nike Swoosh logo by then graduate design student Caroline Davidson to Nike corporate titan Phil Knight for $35.

*Relevance to You:* MS-DOS marks the beginning of a series of popular refrains:

- Microsoft isn't good; they're lucky.
- Microsoft isn't good; they rob, cheat, and steal.
- Microsoft isn't made up of great engineers; they bully, cajole, and walk all over the competition to get what they want.

It is this attitude that eventually engenders lawsuits, anti-trust filings, and Bill Gates getting a pie in the face in Antwerp and shot in the head to great applause in the kiddie musical for grown-ups, *South Park*.

## The Macintosh: 1984

Super Bowl, 1984. A lone runner rushes into a crowded auditorium and hurls an anvil at the monolithic computer screen. The screen is smashed into tiny pieces. The Macintosh is born. The importance of the first affordable personal computer to have a Graphical User Interface (GUI) cannot be underestimated.

## Three Major Developments That Brought Us the World Wide Web

### I. ARPANET

In theory, technologies developed by the Department of Defense (DOD) and NASA are supposed to trickle down to the average citizen. NASA, well, they gave us Tang. And the DOD, aside from a very large stockpile of nuclear weapons and some really great planes that none

## » Two Laws That Govern Computer Development and the Internet

### Moore's Law

*Prior to the notion of Internet time,[13] Moore's Law, named for Gordon Moore, founder of Intel, had been the basis of all developments in Silicon Valley. Moore's Law states that the pace of microchip technology change is such that the amount of data storage a microchip can hold doubles every year, or at least every eighteen months. More data storage means more calculations per second. More calculations per second means faster and faster programs. Faster and faster programs means more complicated computers and software. More complicated computers and software means more product bought and greater riches accrued.*

### »The Line on Moore's Law:

*It is the driving force behind all computer development to date.*

### »The Geek Line on Moore's Law:

*The über-geek line on Moore's Law is that it may be butting up against the laws of physical possibility. Chip designers deal at the atomic layer of existence, and even Gordon Moore himself suggested that by 2017, barring a radical change in microprocessor science, his law will no longer be applicable.*

### Metcalfe's Law

*Bob Metcalfe, inventor of ethernet and founder of 3Com (they're the ones behind the Palm Pilot craze), said that a network's worth is directly related to the number of people on the network. In the language of math, his law says, "Where N is the number of nodes, the power of a network is N squared."*

---

13. Defining Internet time is difficult, as it is highly subjective, and it changes on an almost daily basis, but suffice it to say that six months is a very long time in Internet time. In six months companies lose billions of dollars in their valuation, some go out of business, and others that were but an idea on a piece of paper are the leaders in a sector that previously hadn't even existed.

of us are qualified to see, let alone fly in—well, thanks to the DOD we have the Internet.

At the height of the Cold War, the Advanced Research Projects Agency (ARPA) was contracted by the DOD to come up with a nuke-proof way to communicate, in case, of—well, y'know, the big one. They came up with ARPANET, a primitive way to exchange e-mail.

*What's It to You*: Understand that ARPANET is the beginning. Without ARPANET there is no Internet.

## 2. The World Wide Web

Tim Berners Lee is generally considered to be the father of the World Wide Web, which is the thing most people think of when they think of the Internet. The Internet is the network of networks that connects everything. The Web is the graphical wrapping that makes use of the network infrastructure that is the Internet.

In 1989 Berners Lee was working at a place called CERN in Geneva, Switzerland, and was frustrated by having to reformat, reorganize, and clean up information when it was exchanged from computer to computer. So, over the course of about a year, he wrote a program that allowed for exchanging documents.

*The Spirit behind It All*: Though with each passing day it becomes more difficult to imagine, the Web was truly spawned from an academic mind-set. It sprang forth from a "Gee, wouldn't it be great if I could just communicate with my colleagues in Germany" kind of thing. Think of this notion: "If you can keep your head about you when all others are losing theirs . . ." by Kipling. It will calm you as dot.com hype continues to mount.

## 3. Mosaic, Marc Andreessen, and the Beginning of the Web as We Know It

Marc Andreessen was a little-known grad student at the University of Illinois Champaign-Urbana campus, who, along with six other young programmers, worked on a little program called Mosaic. The program created a Graphical User Interface (GUI) for browsing, putting a "human" face on Tim Berners Lee's World Wide Web. As the story goes, Andreessen moved west, had a meeting with Jim Clark, and next thing you know 65 million people had downloaded the next version of Mosaic—Netscape Navigator.

*The Tech Guy:* Every start-up needs three things: the money guy, the tech guy, and the idea guy. Each of these guys speaks to a different constituency, each of which is vital to the success of the start-up. As programmers go—and these things tend to be a matter of public record—Andreessen is hailed as being good but not great, and certainly not the best ever. He was simply the "tech guy" Jim Clark needed for his new venture. It just so happened that the venture helped reshape the world as we know it.

## Silicon Valley Culture

Why Silicon? Because it's the stuff they use to make those nifty little semiconductors that are at the base of all computing. Silicone is the stuff they put into breasts before it was determined that it might not be the very best of ideas.

## The Importance of "The Garage"

It used to be when people thought "garage" they thought "garage band." The garage plays a very specific and important part in the mythmaking that has sprung up around the heroes of the Silicon Valley and the companies they founded.

The whole garage thing began in 1938 with two guys named Hewlett (William R.) And Packard (David) who, instead of going east to work for establishment companies, set up shop in a little garage at 367 Addison in Palo Alto, California.

Their first client was a small animation company run by a man named Walt Disney, who was then hard at work on a piece of animation called *Fantasia*.

Other famous garages include but are not limited to: the garage in which Steve Jobs and Steve Wozniak built the first Apple computers, and the garage that housed the five guys working on a project they called Architext, which would go on to become Excite.

The late-nineties version of the garage is the large, drafty, industrial loft-space with wall-to-wall Macs and a T3[14] connection.

## The Boys in the Valley

Millionaires and billionaires have sprouted like mushrooms after rain in the late nineties, but here's the short list of some of the major dudes.

---

14. T3 is the bandwidth usually reserved for connecting an ISP (Internet service provider) to the Backbone. (The Backbone is the name used for the main lines that run across the country connecting all of the smaller regions.)

## Steve Jobs: The Visionary

Jobs was the cool geek. The stylish one, Jobs was known to dream in big, wide, materially rewarding canvasses. He even got it right more than once. He got it right with Apple, becoming fabulously wealthy at the age of twenty-six, and then he got it right again with Pixar, the producers of *Toy Story.* And at the end of the 1990s he even got Apple right a second time by rescuing the company from the dead, and disproving all those who said, "You can't go home again."

### » The Take-Away:

When discussing Jobs there is one feature of his personality that is documented and worthy of note. He is known for projecting what is referred to as a "reality distortion field." In other industries this might be characterized as "charisma" or its cousin, "salesmanship," but this is the land of high-tech so it gets a fancy high-tech name.

The reality distortion field is said to have no boundaries; it works in tête-à-têtes as well as company meetings. The concept is something that can and should be invoked in moments when you are experiencing wholesale disbelief, especially if somebody is trying to put one over on you. You might try, "What, do you think you've got some kind of reality distortion field that makes you think I'll believe that?"

### » The Bite-Sized Jobs

In exhorting his minions to do without sleep and create the most fabulous products ever, Jobs urged them to be "insanely great."

When asked about Microsoft in the mid-eighties, he said simply, "Microsoft has no taste."

## Jim Clark: The Entrepreneur

Jim Clark represents a totally unique and original kind of success. He's not a wunderkind—he didn't found his first company until he was in his *late* thirties. That was Silicon Graphics, but once he had that taken care of he went on a roll, founding Netscape (essentially launching the e-economy), and then founding Healtheon because he felt he could revolutionize health care.

*Why You Should Care*: Because Jim Clark has had the kind of success and career that people model their whole lives after? *Nope.* Because he made a call to Marc Andreessen and hatched Netscape, a company that came out of nowhere to bring the Internet to the masses and Microsoft to its knees? *Nope.*

Because, in the words of writer Michael Lewis, Clark represents a new kind of economic man, the billion-dollar idea man, whose ideas are so powerfully simple that entire economies get uprooted and fortunes built on the edifice of his scribbles? *Yep.*

## John Doerr: The Venture Capitalist

John Doerr is a venture capitalist. In some books, he is *the* venture capitalist (VC). He works at the firm of Kleiner, Perkins, Caufield and Byers (KPCB), which is where start-ups go to get their funding. They then build out their product, lose hundreds of millions of dollars, and have an initial public offering (IPO).

John Doerr says things like "We're responsible for the single greatest legal creation of wealth in the history of mankind."

*That Whole Japanese Thing:* Silicon Valley is very into Japanese culture; they admire the focus, they respect the drive, they seek to emulate the organization.

Doerr espouses the notion of *keiretsu*. In Japanese, *keiretsu* refers to a network of companies working together by mutual obligation; in other words, it's a Japanese term for "We're all in this together." It's a fancy way of saying "We put money into your company and we put money into their company and we make much more money if you two companies now work together."

## Paul Allen: The Other Microsoft Founder

He's not in the Valley but he is the cool one, relatively speaking. Since leaving Microsoft for health reasons in 1983, Allen has been living the high life that only the second-richest man at Microsoft could afford. He owns the Portland Trailblazers, the Seattle Seahawks, a $500 million piece of Dreamworks SKG, and he hired architect du moment Frank Gehry to build the $100 million Experience Music Project devoted to Jimi Hendrix.

*The Line on the Man They Call Big Paulie:* He lives with his mom—in the second-biggest house in Seattle, and has the biggest, most kick-ass parties in the world.

Allen invites everyone from Bill Gates to Peter Gabriel on a cruise for three to five days of nonstop partying and picks up the tab. His are some of the most elite parties one could possibly attend. So when the conversation turns to discussions of parties that you haven't been invited to or would like to be invited to, "I just want to go to one of those Paul Allen parties where they cruise the Bering Straits" is a more than appropriate riposte.

## Jerry Yang and David Filo: Procrastination Has Its Rewards

As a side project while pursuing their Ph.D.s in electrical engineering, Jerry and David (it's very much a first-name thing) surfed the Web—a lot! Then at some point their project turned into an index of all the Websites extant, and from there into a "portal," and from there into a full-blown "media brand," which they called YAHOO (Yet Another Hierarchical Officious Oracle).

*Their Relevance:* Because if anybody could actually be said not to care about being a billionaire, it is these two guys. Jerry and David are the cuddliest billionaires since people started keeping track of things like billions of dollars.

# Four Fast Facts

## A Cautionary Tale: Pointcast.com

Everybody has heard the tales of the young, rich entrepreneurs worth hundreds of millions of dollars. People tend not to talk about the ones who missed their moment, but they're out there, and Pointcast is one of them.

It's March 1997 and the hottest thing on the Web is something called "push" technology. The leader by far is Pointcast; it's on everyone's desktops and everybody's lips. Rupert Murdoch offers in the neighborhood of $400 million for the company. Pointcast, thinking they might fare better in a public market or find a higher bidder, turns him down.

Flash to 1999. Pointcast is sold for about $10 million to a company called IdeaLab!

*The Point*: Whenever anyone brags about how much money they turned down for their company, you can shake your head and throw out that index finger, admonishing, "Just remember Pointcast. Just remember Pointcast." This is also a very good way to define hubris in the new media age. "You want hubris? I'll give you hubris: Pointcast turning down four hundred million dollars."

## The Importance of the Employee Number

In Silicon Valley, or really in all start-ups, there is little that is more important than the employee number, as in "He was employee number four." This number determines how many stock options the employee receives, and with stock options worth more than their weight in gold, this is a highly relevant number.

While it would be impolite to ask somebody directly, you may, in conversation, overhear, "He was employee three at Infoseek." This is meant to impress you. Smile knowingly and exclaim, "Wow."

Employee numbers can be represented in quirky yet oddly meaningful ways by what phone extension you have, your parking place, your proximity to a window . . . you get the idea.

## One Great Hoax and One Great Internet Moment

*The Moment When Reality Ceased to Matter*

Summer 1997: An e-mail circulated by friends, colleagues, and family members claimed its origin to be the commencement speech given by Kurt Vonnegut, Jr., at MIT.

The e-mail began simply enough with a Vonnegut-like admonition to "wear sunscreen." It then went on to dispense advice, offer witticisms, and proffer notions on personal conduct, which, to the average observer, passed for that unique Vonnegut flair. However, these wise words were not a commencement speech, nor were they penned by Kurt Vonnegut, Jr. They came from a newspaper column written by a woman named Mary Smich.

*What's It to You*: Even when it became clear that Vonnegut hadn't authored it, the missive continued to make the rounds to an ever-larger audience. Even if it wasn't written by the master satirist, *it might just as well have been,* was how people looked at it.

It defined the Internet culture in a specific fashion wherein half-truths are not really a problem and "truth" is as elusive as it is in "real life." Think of it as a defining moment:

"The moment the Internet found its internal compass, and its internal compass is definitely surreal, was with that whole Kurt Vonnegut commencement speech thing."

## Broadband: It's Heeeeeeere. . . .

The word *broadband* will be thrown around a lot in the next few years. It means high bandwidth—Internet through fast phone lines (DSL) and cable (cable modems). For the layperson this translates to video. For the quasi sophisticate, this translates to a hybrid of video mixed with telephone/chat and interactivity. "Choose the camera-angle view you want to see Mike Tyson get pummeled" and "Vote on whether Heather should go all the way with Bobby or dump him and go with Troy."

When talk turns to broadband, and it will, just as talk has turned to Internet portals, mobile phones, and an auction market developed solely to satiate one woman's quest for Pez dispensers,[15] remember the following experience:

## » The Victoria's Secret Simulcast

In February of 1999, Victoria's Secret simulcast their "fashion show" on the Internet. This revolutionary experience featured grainy video at ten frames per second (this translates to herky-jerky nearly stop-motion quality), and was delivered to tens of thousands of Web surfers (hundreds of thousands were shut out) before the servers crashed.

*What It Means to You*: Borrow liberally from media critic Michael Wolff's interpretation of this event: "I think you have to remember that the Internet never works. We have created the fastest-growing industry in history . . . on the basis of technology which in almost every instance is at least a disappointment and fairly often a catastrophe." (Actually this is applicable to everything having to do with the Internet—save e-mail.)

---

15. The Internet site eBay was started by Pierre Omidyar in an effort to help his wife with her Pez collection.

## Geek Glossary

» *The Borg*—Valley culture is steeped in *Star Trek* lore. And the Borg, the cold, heartless humanity-extinguishing enemy of the crew of *Star Trek: The Next Generation*, is commonly meant to mean Microsoft.

The similarities are striking. In the Borg, individuality and innovation are frowned upon in order to be a part of the greater Borg. At Microsoft, innovation happens by accident and individuality is subsumed into the greater corporate culture, both of which are assimilated into the all-encompassing Windows empire for the greater good of the stock price. In both cases, "Resistance is futile."

» *Burn Rate*—The amount of dollars a start-up burns as it makes its way, in theory, to profitability. The burn comes from the image of burning dollars. The Internet has given new meaning to the statement "It takes money to make money."

Conversational Opportunity: When speaking with somebody who says "I work for an Internet start-up," feel free to say, "What's your burn rate?" It's a little off-putting, perhaps, but it gets the cards on the table pretty quickly.

» *Grok*—To get it. In a technical way. Operable as both a question and a statement. Comes from Robert A. Heinlein's *Stranger in a Strange Land*, wherein it is a Martian term for "to drink" or "to be one with." "Do you grok it?" or "I grok it."

» *Killer App*—The killer app is the thing that everybody wants and nobody knows what it is. The killer app is the hit movie, top-rated TV show, and best-seller all rolled into one. As far as the Internet goes, e-mail is the killer app.

» *Kludge*—Fixing old car-door handles with plastic straws, using duct tape for most anything, writing a software program that can deal with 1,000 queries a second but not 10,000 (when eventually you will of course get 10,000) are all examples of a kludge. A clever technical solution to make something work, by its very nature temporary, though not ephemeral.

Ongoing debate as to whether it is pronounced kluj or klooj.

Conversational Opportunity: Any fix that is temporary, from using a paper clip to keep your eyeglasses together to writing a few thousand lines of code to keep your PC from booting up with the "Battle Hymn of the Republic."

» *Off-Line*—People in meetings who want to discuss something outside of the meeting say "Let's take this off-line." While acceptable as a level of discourse in the company of colleagues, if you hear someone say "Let's take this off-line" outside of cubicle land, you should flee—quickly.

If, however, you are this person's friend, take him politely aside and suggest that if he does anything like that again, he will have to have a Time-Out.

» *Rebel Alliance*—A "below the radar" undercurrent in the Valley similar to the Borg is the notion of the "Rebel Alliance."

Taking a cue from the *Star Wars* movies, the battle to defeat Microsoft is cast as the Rebels vs. the Empire, in which the Rebels are companies such as Oracle, Sun, AOL, IBM, and AT&T—basically everybody but Microsoft.

All non-employees of Microsoft urge each other to work together with the mantra "What's good for the Rebel Alliance is bad for the Empire."

» *URL*—You Are Ell. Might rhyme with hurl, but probably not. The address for a Website, like http://www.onepartkafka.com/computers.html.

» *User Interface* (UI)—The way you interact with information, be it your VCR controls, the window controls in your car, or your refrigerator control knobs. When you are frustrated with the controls of a game, car stereo, remote control, or doorknob, you may, if you so choose, say, "Bad UI."

» *WYSIWYG*—(Pronounced WIZ-ee-wig) What You See Is What You Get. Dates back to when you didn't know how something would look when you went to print it out.

# Required Reading

Non-Fiction

*Burn Rate: How I Survived the Gold Rush Years on the Internet,* by Michael Wolff
A name-dropping firsthand account of the madness that was Internet Gold Rush Phase I. Mixing humor with hubris, this is the book to read and to recommend for the flavor of greed and insanity that marked the start of the Internet Revolution.

*The New New Thing,* by Michael Lewis
Taking Jim Clark of Netscape as a starting point, Lewis paints the picture of Silicon Valley in the late 1990s as a time of economic and technological miracles. The title alone speaks volumes on the necessity of staying ahead of the curve.

Fiction

*Neuromancer,* by William Gibson
*Snow Crash,* by Neil Stephenson
Because everybody who's not a suit has read these two books and in one way or another envisions themselves as hacker superheroes jacking into a brave new world as they write the code for the next big thing.

## Epitaph for the Wired World

Tired of all the relentless boosterism of the Internet Age? Think of how it all might be looked upon in another 500 years. E.g., ". . . and they thought that connecting everybody would be a *good* idea."

# Toasts around the World

*Everyone eventually settles into a particular way to raise a glass.*
*Then again, variety is the spice of life. Rotate as you see fit.*

Chinese

> Mandarin *Gan bei* "Dry your cup!"
> Cantonese *Yam sing* "Dry your cup!"

French

> *À la tienne* (A la tee-yen) As in "To your health" (collo-
> quial). Also available in non-colloquial: *À la Votre.*
> *Santé* Literally translated, "Health."

German

> *Prost* or *Prosit* (Prosnt) "To your health."

Irish/Gaelic

> *Slainte* (Shlantay) "To your health."

Japanese

> *Banzai* "May you live a thousand years."
> *Kampai* (kahm-pie) "Dry cup!"

Russian

> *Za vashe zdorovye* "To your health."

Spanish

> *Salud!* "To your health."

Swedish

> Skäl (shköl) Literally means "Drinking vessel."

Yiddish/Hebrew

> *L'chaim* "To Life."

# THE STREET

"The Internet changes everything."

—Anonymous

 *I could no more teach you about finance than a blind aborigine in Australia could tell you what Buzz Lightyear looks like. But just as knowing something about technology has become a societal survival necessity, so too has having better than passing knowledge about the Financial Markets. Following are the bare-bones basics that might buy you just enough time to say, "Let's talk about something else, shall we?" For after all, there's nothing more crass than talking about money.*

# The Scene

A mere five years ago, rare was the conversation that began with "Have you seen what AOL/YAHOO!/Amazon is at?" But the Internet age has introduced a new virulent addiction into the American mainstream: the stock-market-obsessing, portfolio-watching, personal-wealth-assessing American.

If it *feels* like everyone is "playing the market" these days, it's because they are. Americans placed a record 28 percent of their household wealth in their stock accounts, a *New York Times*[1] study showed—and that was in 1998, before the NASDAQ soared 80 percent through calendar year 1999.

# Know the Markets

### The New York Stock Exchange

The granddaddy of the U.S. Stock Market is the New York Stock Exchange, fondly referred to as "The Big Board." The NYSE dates back to 1792, when twenty-four brokers met under a buttonwood tree. They've been trading every weekday since 1873 (they used to trade on Saturdays) save for a five-month stall during World War I.

### » Some Things to Know about the NYSE

It's an auction market. To trade on the floor, you need to be one of the 1,366 members who have a "seat" (the number of seats has held steady since 1953). In 1998 the price of a seat was anywhere from $1,225,000 to $2,000,000.

---

1. *New York Times*, February 11, 1998, Edward Wyatt, Business/Financial Desk.

Stocks listed on the NYSE are assigned to a specialist who handles the auctions for that particular stock at one of seventeen trading booths on the floor.

## The NASDAQ

### » The NASDAQ Is a Network

The NASDAQ (National Association of Securities Dealers Automated Quotations, formerly the "NASDAQ" system) market doesn't really exist. There's no trading floor per se; the exchange functions electronically.

To show you've been in the market longer than Tiger Woods has been on the PGA, recall the time when the NASDAQ was thought of as the ugly kid brother, the lesser cousin. Then Microsoft (MSFT) went public in 1986 and subsequently skyrocketed to being the largest market cap company in the U.S.A., and NASDAQ overcame any possible case of the inferiority-complex blues.

Other high-fliers listed on the NASDAQ include Intel (INTC) and Cisco (CSCO), who along with Microsoft make up three of the five largest market caps in the world. The coup de grâce is that the NASDAQ is the market of choice for the dot.com world, and it's where you'll find Priceline (PCLN), Amazon (AMZN), and eBay (EBAY).

## The Debt Market: Bonds

Some people spend their whole lives in debt. The diligent among us avoid it. Shakespeare warned us against it. But there are those who buy and sell it for a living. Companies (and governments) issue debt so they can finance projects: a new plant, a dam, or, in the historical case, a war. Just like stocks, these bonds (read: debt) are traded in order to make a profit.[2] (Think of a bond as a great big corporate IOU.)

The major thing to understand about debt is that it is rated (Moody's and Standard & Poor's [S&P] are the

---

## » *Terms for Bonds*

Coupon—*The fixed amount paid out semi-annually (that's two times a year), based on the percentage rate of the bond during the life of the bond. Zero coupon bonds have no payments; a lump sum or balloon payment is paid at the very end.*

Grades—*Standard & Poor's and Moody's rate bonds for safety. For S & P the rates go from AAA to C. For Moody's from Aaa to D.*

Junk Bonds—*If a bond is rated Baa (Moody's) or BBB (S&P), it's "Investment Grade." Ratings of Caa (Moody's) or CCC (S&P) or below are, in the parlance of the eighties, "Junk Bonds" or "High-Yield Bonds," as they belong to riskier companies but offer higher rates.*

Prime—*The Prime Lending Rate. A benchmark around which all other lending rates function.*

Yield—*Know that it's inversely rated to the Price. The higher the price, the lower the yield. The lower the price, the higher the yield.*

---

2. Nick Carraway, the narrator of *The Great Gatsby*, was a bond trader. As he put it so eloquently, "Everybody I knew was in the bond business, so I supposed it could support one more single man."

classic raters). Like schoolkids, companies and governments are given grades—AAA being the highest, down to something you really don't want to know about. The worse the grade, the higher the yield.

## Market Terms

As we have become market obsessed, market terms have become as much (or more) a part of the vocabulary as other, more popular metaphors, like terms pertaining to Sports and War.

» Bear—If the market is down by 20 percent it's considered a bear market. Forms of the word can be employed as both a noun and an adjective. One who is pessimistic about the market may be considered a bear, and if he or she issues a statement, it is "bearish" in tone.

» Bull—When the market is up or headed up, it's a bull market; and when the market is truly soaring, it is a raging bull. "Bull" can also be used out of context. You can be bullish on a person, on a concept, or on Charlie Brown's prospects of finally taking out the cute little redheaded girl. E.g., "I'm bullish on us getting floor seats tonight."

» Blue Chip—Highly valued stocks of large, national companies with steady earnings and potential for growth. This term is useful outside the world of stocks, in referring to artists who have arrived at a certain level of collectibility, high school basketball prospects poised for greatness, and racehorses with excellent pedigrees.

» Long—Holding on to what you have. Essentially, if you buy a stock to hold on to it, you are "long." The funny thing about being long is, in a world where people now hold stocks for fifteen to thirty seconds, laws of relativity mean that being long can mean holding on to something for two full days.

» Options—The right to buy or sell a property that is granted in exchange for a given sum. They come in two flavors:

  • A call lets a person *buy* a stock at a specified price by a specified date.

  • A put lets a person *sell* a stock at a specified price by a specified date.

Know of the existence of the Black-Scholes Formula. Fisher Black and Nobel prize winner Myron Scholes were two guys who came up with an exact way of figuring out just how much options are worth.

» Short—Selling a stock that you don't own under the assumption that it will soon be going down. If, for example, America Online (AOL) was trading at 140 and you think it will go south, you could "short" it, selling what you don't have at 140, and then, when the stock falls, perhaps to 120 or so, you buy it back and pocket the difference.

» The Street—Wall Street, of course. So named due to the location of the trading floor of the NYSE. The Street is the place where it all happens, the center of corporate finance. The goal of most companies is to "beat the street," which means to have greater earnings or slimmer losses than analysts have forecast.

# The Sky Is Falling! The Sky Is Falling!

Three historical instances to invoke the next time the Dow dips 25 percent—and it *will* happen.

## Tulip Mania

It's 1637 and the Dutch economy is in a frenzy. It's not tobacco, it's not diamonds, it's not even tea. It's all about tulips! In seventeenth-century Holland, tulip bulbs became *the* must-have item[3] for the happening Holland-ite. Overpriced at several hundred dollars a pop, tulip bulbs were selling for thousands of dollars per. In the end, the whole thing fell apart and the Dutch economy tanked, nearly bringing down the rest of Europe, or at least London, with it.

With the speculative hype of the Internet, this bit of historical fact-dropping has come back into vogue, tossed off as a bon mot at technology conferences by MIT grads. So when everybody wants the new new thing, no matter what the costs, recite your mantra: "Remember the tulips. Remember the tulips."

## The Crash of 1929

On October 29, 1929, the Dow dropped 11.7 percent of its value. This was the big one. But rest comfortably, secure in the knowledge that it was only one of the many factors contributing to the Great Depression, not the sole

---

3. In modern-day society, there have been isolated outbreaks of similar frenzies. Both the Beanie Baby boom of the mid-1990s and the Pokémon craze at the end of the century bore the same bench-marks of a must-have-at-all-costs frenzy. Not to mention Cabbage Patch Kids, rare-comic-book booms, and, well, baseball cards.

cause. Other factors included poorly regulated banks, the Federal Reserve being tight with the money supply, and the International Monetary System as a whole having a rough time. So fear not that a big dip in the market will necessarily lead to panhandling as a career move.

## The Crash of 1987

Black Monday. The Dow Jones dropped 508.32 points, losing 22.6 percent of its value, and Wall Street laid off 15,000 people. The net effect was that everybody in college at the time who thought they were heading to Wall Street ended up going to law school. Hence the glut of disenchanted lawyers in their thirties looking for different careers. Happily, the Dow took just fourteen months to regain the losses of Black Monday, climbing back to its previous value of 2,256.43 on January 24, 1989.

## The Importance of Alan Greenspan

Alan Greenspan is the chairman of the Federal Reserve Board, and he reigns supreme over the ebb and flow of the money supply, which, in turn, influences interest rates. With higher interest rates, the economy slows; lower interest rates, the economy goes. Therefore, all the world focuses with scrutiny on every utterance from the man's mouth.

The economy is global and with the United States carrying the flag as the world's largest economy, by inference, Alan is "the Man," as in the most powerful man in the Western world.

For the short-attention-span theater crowd.
Remember this one phrase that Greenspan tossed off
one afternoon. He suggested that the mad love affair
with the late-nineties market was characterized by "irra-
tional exuberance."

> *Show you're no johnny-come-lately by fondly recalling the
> cigar-chomping, LBO-fighting, junk-bond-resisting antics
> of Paul Volcker, the head of the Fed under Reagan.*

## A Tale of Two Decades: LBOs and IPOs

Follow the MBA. Follow the MBA. It's the quickest way
to understand where the hottest, most lucrative jobs can
be found. What IPOs and Silicon Valley start-ups have
been to the nineties, LBOs and elite investment firms
were to the eighties.

## Greed I: The 1980s

You remember the eighties. Madonna sang "Material
Girl." Oliver Stone made *Wall Street* with that infamous
line "Greed is good." And a man named Michael Milken
pulled down $550 million in one year, prompting out-
rage, indignation, and no less a paragon of humility than
Donald Trump to say, "You can be happy on a lot less
money."[4] Most of all, mergers and acquisitions were
turning the financial markets upside down, and the Wall
Street elite were cashing in.

---

4. *New York Times,* April 3, 1989, Metropolitan Desk.

It was a colorful swaggering time, different from the nineties baby billionaires living in their grad-student bachelor pads and driving Hondas. It was a time for living large, and these were some of the largest.

---

### » MBASpeak for the Eighties

*EBITDA (EE-bit-da)*[5]
*Earnings Before Interest, Taxes, Depreciation, and Amortization, a term that Mergers and Acquisitions (M&A) folks adore. In short, what earnings would be if you didn't have to pay all those messy depreciation costs. It's a proxy for cash flow. A finance guy at a tech company might say something like "Of course we don't focus on EBITDA; we're looking at the top-line numbers."*

*NPV (EN-pee-vee)*
*Net Present Value, the true intrinsic value of any corporation or project. It's a calculation that is usually accomplished by hordes of bookish-looking people dressed in gray, eating really bad Chinese on a deserted floor of a global megacorp.*

*LBOs (El-BEE-oohs)*
*The hottest thing on Wall Street in the 1980s. Young financial whizzes were banging down the door to get into Drexel Burnham Lambert,[6] where Michael Milken hung his hat, and set to work in the M&A department—that's pronounced EM-en-AY.*

---

5. Fans of the late-seventies TV show *Taxi* might recall the character Latka Gravas as played by the comedian/performance artist Andy Kaufman. His two catchphrases were "Thank you very much" and "Ibida," the latter being a nonsensical word in a nonsensical language that Kaufman had made up for the character. EBITDA is pronounced in just the same way as Ibida.
6. There are legions of people who claim to have been offered a job at Drexel before it went under. This is similar to "Harrison Ford was my carpenter" and "I was at Woodstock."

## » MBASpeak for the Eighties (continued)

*In a Leveraged Buy-Out, Investor X wants to buy Public Company B, which is worth about $10 billion, but he doesn't have the cash to do it. He goes to a firm like Drexel and says, "Hey, I want to buy that company over there and I've got one billion dollars. Will you sell nine billion in bonds [see above] so that I can do it?" Drexel says sure. The buy-out goes through, the shareholders receive their portion of the $10 billion, and Investor X now owns a company, a company with $9 billion worth of debt.*

*P/E (PEE-ee)*
*The Price-to-Earnings ratio is a different kind of metric for measuring the value of a company. Yet for companies that have little to no earnings, P/E is little more than a charming relic of some antiquarian investing past.*

*Risk Arbitrage*
*A technique used by alert traders to profit from minute price differences for the same security on different markets. For example, if a computer monitoring markets notices that ABC stock can be bought on a New York exchange for $10 a share and sold on a London exchange at $10.12, the arbitrageur can simultaneously purchase ABC stock in New York while selling the same amount of it in London, pocketing the difference. It's what Ivan Boesky did.*

# The Very Definition of Living Large

## The Prototype: Sir James Goldsmith

Along with his accomplice Al "Chainsaw" Dunlap, Sir James was the prototypical corporate raider, buying up companies like Crown Zellerbach and slicing them into little pieces. To their critics Dunlap said, "We were operating on sick companies, cutting out the cancer."

Any conversation having to do with alternative and/or extravagant lifestyles by necessity has to touch on Sir James. The highlights of his extremely colorful bio include but are not limited to: winning $8,000 on a horse race at Eton when he was sixteen years old, eloping with a Bolivian tin heiress at age twenty, and selling out of the market prior to the crash in 1987.

He had three wives, eight children, and properties in Mexico, New York, Spain, Paris, and London. The mistresses, of course, knew about the wives, and more interestingly the wives knew about the mistresses.

## Risk Arbitrageur Goes from Hero to Zero: Ivan Boesky

Along with Milken, he paid the price for being the face on greed. Most remembered for paying a $100 million fine, his jail term wherein he grew a Methuselah-like beard, and—oh yes, getting caught completely red-handed for the practice of insider trading.

### » Cheese Points:

It was Boesky's speech at a Berkeley MBA commencement that inspired the character of Gordon Gekko in

Oliver Stone's *Wall Street*. In his speech Boesky said, "I think greed is healthy. You can be greedy and still feel good about yourself."

## "Hey, It's Not *All* My Fault": Michael Milken

"Mr. Milken's compensation, which topped $550 million in 1987 alone, exceeded $1 billion in a four-year period. Surely no one in American history has earned anywhere near as much in a year as Mr. Milken, head of the high-yield bond department at Drexel Burnham Lambert, Inc. J. P. Morgan, the best-known financier of this century, had a total net worth of less than $500 million when he died in 1913, and even allowing for inflation his income never matched Mr. Milken's."
—*New York Times*, April 3, 1989

An acknowledged financial genius who along with Boesky got into a little trouble for having his hand in the cookie jar, Milken has spent the time since getting out of jail trying to prove that he's not such a bad guy after all, raising dollars and awareness for cancer and turning the education market on its head by suggesting that the children of America might be better served if education was a privately run enterprise.

Milken was the ringleader of the 1980s high-wire financial circus. He provides a fascinating dose of perspective, though. As detailed above, Milken was paid $550 million in 1987 for services rendered to Drexel Burnham Lambert. But now, with billionaires popping up overnight, this achievement seems almost quaint. "Oh look, Martha, Mikey earned $550 million."

The interesting thing about Milken is that he remains close with all his colleagues from the eighties. When Ted Turner sold Turner Broadcasting to Time Warner, Milken was given a $550 million consulting fee. Which just gives one pause: What kind of *consulting* results in those kinds of fees?

## Greed II: The 1990s

### Let's Go IPO, Everybody's Going IPO, Won't You Go IPO with Me?

So while the big game in the 1980s was elite, shrewd, and greedy financiers putting together elaborate financing schemes to purchase undervalued companies, the nineties game is to put together elaborately crafted companies that will "capitalize on future revenue streams made possible by the Internet." In other words, the goal is to create companies that might be profitable one day but there's not necessarily any way to tell if they will, and anybody who says they know is lying.

## Here's How It's Done:

- Write a business plan, making sure it has something to do with the Internet. Score bonus points for a generic name with a ".com" suffix (like soap.com or pencil.com). Extra bonus points for clever name adapted from ancient Greek or some equally obscure language.
- Be in business for about six months and lose at least $15 million on revenues of $20,000, or realize no revenues whatsoever.
- Raise money from Menlo Park–based venture capital firm. Be sure it has a Sandhill Road address.
- Hire an investment bank to underwrite your IPO and take your story on the "road show." While the road show's purpose is to raise interest in your IPO, be sure to jot down particularly stressful or funny events as they happen. Road-show stories are great conversation starters (as in "I remember one time on the road show when . . .").
- Give "Friends and Family" stock at the IPO price to make sure they always have nice things to say about you.
- Go public and watch your stock triple in one day—become a paper multimillionaire.

## IPO Terms

» The Float—The float is the number of shares available to the trading public. The smaller the float, the more volatile the stock.

» Flipping—When a stock opens on its first day of trading, those who have purchased the stock at its offering price will "flip" the stock, meaning they will sell it off immediately into the public market.

» Lock-Up Period—The period of time during which company employees cannot sell following the IPO, usually six months. Can be problematic as share prices dive.

» Market Cap—Take the price per share, multiply by the number of shares in the company, and you have the market cap or capitalization. This is relevant to the Internet world because it is those companies' indomitable market caps that allow them to run around and buy up other companies with their incredibly supercharged stocks. Also good party fodder: "What's your market cap?"

» Quiet Period—The time during which a company can't talk publicly about what they're up to. Post filing with the SEC to take a company public.

» Strike Price—The price at which an Investment Bank prices the IPO to open.

» Moonshot—When a stock jumps through the roof upon going public.

## Bill Gates Is *Not* the Richest American in History

Taking the rich down a notch is as American a pastime as baseball. John D. Rockefeller and Cornelius Vanderbilt were much abused in their day, Howard Hughes has been dragged through the mud long since he slipped this mortal coil, and heckling Bill Gates in all his billionaire-geek glory has only gotten pettier as his wealth has eclipsed anything beyond human imagination. *The New Yorker* even took a gratuitous swipe at His Billness when, in one of those voluminous 40,000-word pieces that feel more like a small novel than a magazine article, the writer suggested that Gates's characteristic rocking motion[7] was a sign that he is "borderline autistic."

Yet, while Bill Gates is the richest man alive today, he is not the richest man ever, nor even the richest man in American history. That honor goes to fellow monopolist John D. Rockefeller, who, at the peak of his fiduciary life in 1913, was worth an estimated $900 million, or about $189.6 billion when adjusted for inflation. Here's a quick chart to show you that Bill still has some ground to make up if he's going to qualify as the richest American ever.

---

7. Despite being phenomenally wealthy, Gates is best remembered for three very specific trademarks: his V-neck sweaters, his childlike voice with a bubble in the middle of it, and the rocking motion he falls into when he speaks. (In Yiddish they would call it *davening*.)

| RICH GUY | DOLLARS—ENW[8] | DOLLARS TODAY | GNP/ENW[9] |
|---|---|---|---|
| John D. Rockefeller 1839–1937 | $900 million | $189.6 billion | 44 |
| Andrew Carnegie 1835–1919 | $250 million | $100.5 billion | 83 |
| Cornelius Vanderbilt 1794–1877 | $105 million | $95.9 billion | 87 |
| Bill Gates 1955–? | $78 billion | $78 billion | 108 |

» What's It to You:

It's all relative. And yes, Bill Gates is rich, but at this point he's chasing history, and historically he still has a long way to go.

## Required Reading

*Den of Thieves,* by James B. Stewart

Detailing the labyrinthine path of corruption and hubris that led to the downfall of Messrs. Milken, Boesky, and Levine. A beat reporter in the early 1980s for *The Wall Street Journal,* Stewart had the inside skinny on the

---

8. Estimated Net Worth.
9. If you take the GNP of the nation and divide it by the Estimated Net Worth of the individual, you get a better idea of just how rich, relative to the size of the national economy, this person is/was.

tangled web of arbitrage, junk bonds, and LBOs. A snapshot in history detailing unabashed avarice, remarkable greed, and vertiginous falls. See also *Barbarians at the Gate*, by Bryan Burrough and John Heylar.

## Liar's Poker, by Michael Lewis

Act I when re-inventing oneself: Write a book. Similar in take to the Hollywood tell-all, fair-haired wonder boy Lewis details his rise from lackey to big-time bond salesman, with wonder and bemusement all the way. The title, for those who don't know, refers to the boyish game of playing poker with the serial numbers of hundred-dollar bills.

## The Bonfire of the Vanities, by Tom Wolfe

Gave the world the line "Masters of the Universe," in reference to the bond traders of Wall Street. Yeah, it's fiction, but with a neo-realist gleam. If the idea of reading non-fiction about finance causes a brain-freeze similar to what happens when you drink an Icee too fast, check out *Bonfire*. And for those who can't be bothered, there is a remarkably simple moral to it: If you lose the money and the apartment, you lose the upper-crust friends, too. It's a package deal.

# BEHAVIORAL NOTES

*A few maxims to keep floating in the back of your head as you make your way through an evening.*

- If there are name tags and it's not a fund-raiser, leave.
- If you don't feel up to speaking, be hostile and/or cryptic. Open hostility is often mistaken for genius.
- Make veiled references to Noam Chomsky whenever possible.
- If asked a question relating to religion to which you don't really have a clear-cut answer, respond, "I believe in the interconnectedness of all things."
- If somebody mentions "deconstruction," reel off the following sentence: "Oh yeah, that whole Derrida, Foucalt, Lacan thing." Nobody actually really understands it, so this will pass for erudition.
- If the music sucks, feel free to change it.
- Regardless of how excellent your parking space is, more than one comment per evening relating to "parking karma" is superfluous.
- When all else fails, compliment their shoes.
- Unless it is a Martini Party, do not order one. The proper ingredients and care required to make a martini are not necessarily present at all functions, and one should not assume that just because alcohol is being served one can obtain a martini.

- When seated next to several guests all hovering over hot food that nobody is eating, announce that "Emily Post said you can begin when three are served." This will either endear you to your fellow starving dinner guests or bring about a conversation regarding whether this is true or not that should eat up the time until all have been served.
- Dress nicely, bring gifts—the later you arrive, the more nattily you should be attired. And the later you arrive, the greater the bounty you should have in your possession.
- Know of at least one below-the-radar civil war. These can usually be found on page eight of the "World" section of the *New York Times*. It bespeaks a certain worldliness as regards international politics, human rights, and your concern for things outside your realm of experience.
- Don't play the name game in vain. If you have failed in your first three attempts—college, summer camp, and the winter you spent in Jackson—move on to other fields of interest, like favorite sports teams.
- If you feel like disparaging someone, say, "They say he killed a man." It worked like a charm in *Gatsby*.

# The Exit (or How to Avoid the Thirty-Five-Minute Goodbye)

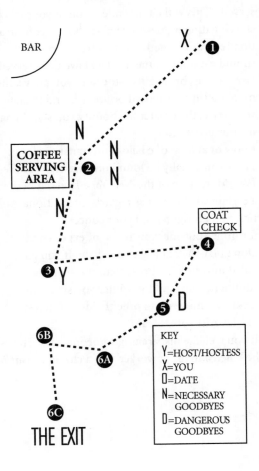

# THE EXIT

1. Assume leaving will require at least one-half hour. Recognize that accomplishing this task in less than thirty minutes will put you in the bonus round. (Note: People with children are able to leave at any time they choose—understand that this, while having its own drawbacks, does seem to come in handy during the exit process.)

2. While it is never too early to begin saying goodbye, Over Coffee is the first prime opportunity to begin the departure drill, toss off a few selective Necessary Goodbyes. If you are truly pressed, the moment the notion of coffee is suggested is when you can begin your egress. From this moment on all energy can and should be directed toward the exit.

3. Seek out the host or hostess to say thank you. This is the sole necessary task of the evening—and, once this is done, all other "au revoirs" are merely grace-notes on a successful departure.

4. Grab your coats. Once in hand, the air of readiness that you project will be difficult for even the most long-winded Dangerous Goodbye artist to overcome.

5. Employ the placing of the coat upon your date's shoulder as an offensive ploy to separate him/her from a Dangerous Goodbye.

6. Execute three necessary goodbyes—colleague/in-law/running partner—to show commitment to the goodbye process. Choose these goodbyes based on the criteria of proximity to the door and minimal time to complete the action. Having undertaken this absolute minimum you have fulfilled the myriad obligations of the evening and can now exit into the starlit evening.

The author wishes to acknowledge that the following books were used as references in the writing of *The Portable Pundit*:

*The Dictionary of Cultural Literacy*
E.D. Hirsch, Jr., Joseph F. Kett, and James Trefil
(Houghton Mifflin, 1993).

*An Incomplete Education*
Judy Jones, William Wilson
(Ballantine Books, 1995).

*Barron's Dictionary of Finance and Investment Terms 5th Edition*
John Downes, Elliot Goodman,
and Jordan Elliot Goodman
(Barron's, 1998).

*New Larousse Encyclopedia of Mythology*
Robert Graves
(out of print).

*Learning from Las Vegas: The Forgotten Symbolism of Architectural Form*
Revised Edition, Robert Venturi, Denise Scott Brown
(M.I.T. Press, 1977).

*Dictionary of Philosophy and Religion: Eastern and Western Thought*
William L. Reese
(Humanities Press/Harvester Press, 1996).

# REFERENCES

*5001 Nights at the Movies*
Pauline Kael
(Henry Holt, 1991).

*The Film Encyclopedia, 3rd Edition*
Ephraim Katz
(HarperPerennials, 1998).

*The Painted Word*
Tom Wolfe
(Bantam Doubleday Dell, 1976).

*From Bauhaus to Our House*
Tom Wolfe
(Bantam Doubleday Dell, 1999).